COMMON CORE LANGUAGE ARTS 4 Today

Daily Skill Practice

Grade 5

Carson-Dellosa Publishing, LLC
Greensboro, North Carolina

Credits

Content Editors: Nancy Rogers Bosse and Christine Schwab
Copy Editor: Elsbeth Krumholz

 Visit *carsondellosa.com* for correlations to Common Core State, national, and Canadian provincial standards.

Carson-Dellosa Publishing, LLC
PO Box 35665
Greensboro, NC 27425 USA
carsondellosa.com

ISBN 978-1-62442-608-7
03-252131151

Table of Contents

Introduction

Common Core Language Arts 4 Today: Daily Skill Practice is a perfect supplement to any classroom language arts curriculum. Students' reading skills will grow as they work on comprehension, fluency, vocabulary, and decoding. Students' writing skills will improve as they work on elements of writing, writing structure, genre, parts of speech, grammar, and spelling, as well as the writing process.

This book covers 40 weeks of daily practice. Four comprehension questions or writing exercises a day for four days a week will provide students with ample practice in language arts skills. A separate assessment is included for the fifth day of each week.

Various skills and concepts are reinforced throughout the book through activities that align to the Common Core State Standards. To view these standards, please see the Common Core State Standards Alignment Matrix on pages 7 and 8.

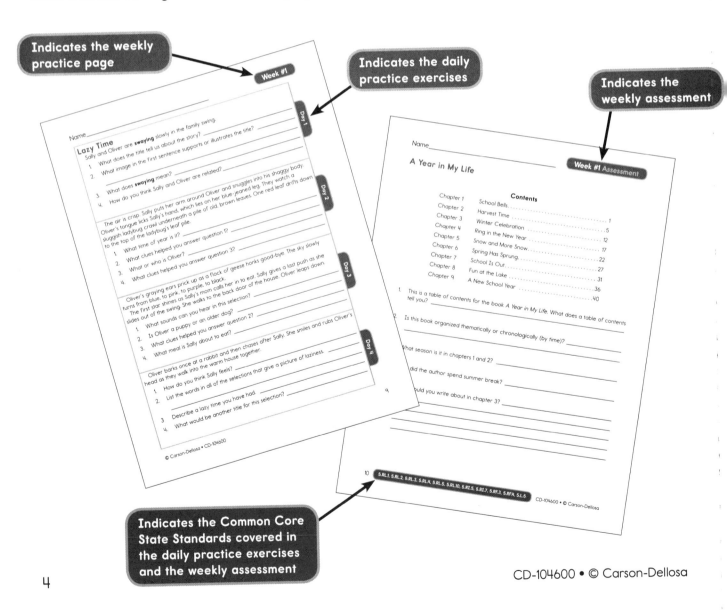

Indicates the weekly practice page

Indicates the daily practice exercises

Indicates the weekly assessment

Indicates the Common Core State Standards covered in the daily practice exercises and the weekly assessment

4

A positive reading environment is essential to fostering successful readers. When building a reading environment, think of students' physical, emotional, and cognitive needs.

Physical Environment

- Make the physical reading environment inviting and comfortable. Create a reading corner with comfortable chairs, floor pillows, a rug, enticing lighting, etc.
- Give students access to a variety of texts by providing books, magazines, newspapers, and Internet access. Read signs, ads, posters, menus, pamphlets, labels, boxes, and more!
- Provide regularly scheduled independent reading time in class. Encourage students to read at home. They can read to a younger sibling or read anything of interest such as comic books, children's and sports magazines, chapter books, etc.
- Set a positive example. Make sure students see you reading too!

Emotional Environment

- Learn about students' reading habits, preferences, strengths, and weaknesses. Then, provide books that address these issues.
- Help students create connections with text. Facilitate connections by activating prior knowledge, examining personal meaning, and respecting personal reflections.
- Give students the opportunity to choose titles to read. This will give them a sense of ownership, which will engage them in the text and sustain interest.
- Create a safe environment for exploring and trying new things. Foster a feeling of mutual respect for reading abilities and preferences.
- Require students to read at an appropriate reading level. Text in any content area, including leisure reading, should not be too easy or too difficult.
- Have all students participate in reading, regardless of their reading levels. Try to include slower readers and be sure to give them time to finish before moving on or asking questions.
- Be enthusiastic about reading! Talk about books you love and share your reading experiences and habits. Your attitude about reading is contagious!

Cognitive Environment

- Regardless of the grade level, read aloud to students every day. Reading aloud not only provides a good example but also lets students practice their listening skills.
- Help students build their vocabularies to make their reading more successful. Create word walls, personal word lists, mini-dictionaries, and graphic organizers.
- Read for different purposes. Reading a novel requires skills that are different from reading an instruction manual. Teach students the strategies needed to comprehend these different texts.
- Encourage students to talk about what and how they read. Use journal writing, literature circles, class discussions, conferences, conversations, workshops, seminars, and more.
- Writing and reading are inherently linked. Students can examine their own writing through reading and examine their reading skills by writing. Whenever possible, facilitate the link between reading and writing.

Writing Strategies

Choose a **topic** for your writing.
- What am I writing about?

Decide on a **purpose** for writing.
- Why am I writing this piece?
- What do I hope the audience will learn from reading this piece?

Identify your **audience**.
- Who am I writing to?

Decide on a writing **style**.
- Expository—gives information or explains facts or ideas
- Persuasive—tries to talk someone into something
- Narrative—tells a story
- Descriptive—presents a clear picture of a person, place, thing, or idea

Decide on a **genre**—essay, letter, poetry, autobiography, fiction, or nonfiction.

Decide on a **point of view**—first person, second person, or third person.

Brainstorm by listing or drawing your main ideas.

Use a graphic organizer to **organize** your thoughts.

Revise, revise, revise!
- Use **descriptive words**.
- Use **transitions** and linking expressions.
- Use a **variety of sentence structures**.
- **Elaborate** with facts and details.
- Group your ideas into **paragraphs**.
- **Proofread** for capitalization, punctuation, and spelling.

CD-104600 • © Carson-Dellosa

Common Core State Standards Alignment Matrix

STANDARD	W1	W2	W3	W4	W5	W6	W7	W8	W9	W10	W11	W12	W13	W14	W15	W16	W17	W18	W19	W20
5.RL.1	●		●		●		●		●		●									
5.RL.2	●		●		●		●		●											
5.RL.3	●		●		●		●		●		●									
5.RL.4	●				●		●		●		●									
5.RL.5	●				●	●					●									
5.RL.6					●						●									
5.RL.7			●																	
5.RL.9			●																	
5.RL.10	●		●		●		●		●		●									
5.RI.1													●		●		●		●	
5.RI.2													●		●		●		●	
5.RI.3													●		●		●		●	
5.RI.4													●		●		●		●	
5.RI.5	●																			
5.RI.6													●		●		●		●	
5.RI.7	●												●		●		●		●	
5.RI.8													●		●		●		●	
5.RI.9													●		●		●		●	
5.RI.10													●		●		●		●	
5.RF.3	●						●				●						●			
5.RF.4	●		●		●		●		●		●		●		●		●		●	
5.W.1				●										●						●
5.W.2		●		●										●				●		
5.W.3				●				●		●		●				●				
5.W.4				●		●	●					●			●		●	●		●
5.W.5				●		●	●						●		●		●	●	●	
5.W.6				●		●	●			●			●		●		●	●		●
5.W.7																	●			
5.W.8																	●			
5.W.9																	●			
5.W.10				●		●		●		●			●		●		●			●
5.L.1		●											●		●		●		●	
5.L.2		●		●		●		●					●		●		●		●	
5.L.3			●		●	●		●			●	●			●	●		●		
5.L.4		●	●				●		●	●	●								●	
5.L.5	●		●			●	●				●									
5.L.6																	●		●	

W = Week

Common Core State Standards Alignment Matrix

STANDARD	W21	W22	W23	W24	W25	W26	W27	W28	W29	W30	W31	W32	W33	W34	W35	W36	W37	W38	W39	W40
5.RL.1																			●	
5.RL.2																			●	
5.RL.3																			●	
5.RL.4																			●	
5.RL.5																			●	
5.RL.6																			●	
5.RL.7																				
5.RL.9																			●	
5.RL.10																			●	
5.RI.1	●		●		●		●		●		●		●		●		●			
5.RI.2	●		●		●		●		●		●		●		●		●			
5.RI.3	●		●		●		●		●		●		●				●			
5.RI.4	●		●		●		●		●		●		●		●		●			
5.RI.5	●		●		●		●		●		●		●				●			
5.RI.6	●		●		●		●		●		●		●				●			
5.RI.7	●		●		●		●		●		●		●				●			
5.RI.8	●		●		●		●		●		●		●				●			
5.RI.9	●		●		●		●		●		●		●				●			
5.RI.10	●		●		●		●		●		●		●		●		●			
5.RF.3	●		●				●		●						●		●		●	
5.RF.4	●		●		●		●		●		●		●		●		●		●	
5.W.1		●																		
5.W.2				●					●				●		●		●		●	●
5.W.3																				
5.W.4		●		●					●				●		●		●		●	●
5.W.5		●		●					●				●		●		●		●	●
5.W.6		●		●					●				●		●		●		●	●
5.W.7				●										●		●		●		●
5.W.8				●										●		●		●		●
5.W.9														●		●		●		●
5.W.10		●		●					●				●		●		●		●	●
5.L.1		●		●		●			●		●		●			●		●		●
5.L.2		●		●		●			●		●		●	●		●		●		●
5.L.3		●	●	●	●		●	●		●		●					●		●	
5.L.4	●				●		●		●		●			●	●	●	●		●	
5.L.5	●								●		●								●	
5.L.6			●						●					●						

W = Week

Lazy Time

Sally and Oliver are **swaying** slowly in the family swing.

1. What does the title tell us about the story? _____

2. What image in the first sentence supports or illustrates the title? _____

   _____

3. What does **swaying** mean? _____

4. How do you think Sally and Oliver are related? _____

The air is crisp. Sally puts her arm around Oliver and snuggles into his shaggy body. Oliver's tongue licks Sally's hand, which lies on her blue-jeaned leg. They watch a sluggish ladybug crawl underneath a pile of old, brown leaves. One red leaf drifts down to the top of the ladybug's leaf pile.

1. What time of year is it? _____

2. What clues helped you answer question 1? _____

3. What or who is Oliver? _____

4. What clues helped you answer question 3? _____

Oliver's graying ears prick up as a flock of geese honks good-bye. The sky slowly turns from blue, to pink, to purple, to black.

The first star shines as Sally's mom calls her in to eat. Sally gives a last push as she slides out of the swing. She walks to the back door of the house. Oliver leaps down.

1. What sounds can you hear in this selection? _____

2. Is Oliver a puppy or an older dog? _____

3. What clues helped you answer question 2? _____

4. What meal is Sally about to eat? _____

Oliver barks once at a rabbit and then chases after Sally. She smiles and rubs Oliver's head as they walk into the warm house together.

1. How do you think Sally feels? _____

2. List the words in all of the selections that give a picture of laziness. _____

   _____

3 Describe a lazy time you have had. _____

4. What would be another title for this selection? _____

A Year in My Life

Contents

1. This is a table of contents for the book *A Year in My Life*. What does a table of contents tell you? _____

2. Is this book organized thematically or chronologically (by time)? _____

    _____

3. What season is it in chapters 1 and 2? _____

4. How did the author spend summer break? _____

5. What would you write about in chapter 3? _____

    _____

    _____

    _____

    _____

 5.RL.1, 5.RL.2, 5.RL.3, 5.RL.4, 5.RL.5, 5.RL.10, 5.RI.5, 5.RI.7, 5.RF.3, 5.RF.4, 5.L.5   CD-104600 • © Carson-Dellosa

Correct the errors in each sentence.

1. Today, dad and i are going to the Park.

2. Its the Great Junkyard Racecar Day!

3. The fifth graders racecars had to be built using junk.

4. I can't weight to see whose racing first!

Day 1

Correct the errors in each sentence.

1. the first group to race will be benjamin's Group.

2. My favorite teacher, Ms. Daniels, was their to.

3. Oh, no! The cars wheels fell off. Thats too bad.

4. Witch car is your favourite?

Day 2

Correct the errors in each sentence.

1. Wow, Mrs. nguyen's Kindergarten class is at the race too.

2. Is that you're sister over they're?

3. It looks like theyre making repairs to the cars front end.

4. That's becuz the car is going to fall a part.

Day 3

Correct the errors in each sentence.

1. did you see mr. Garcia's red car in the race?

2. Its the fastest car in the race.

3. Im going to build the fastest car for next years race.

4. Mom was pleazed and surprized that my sister's car stayed in one peace.

Day 4

Use proofreading marks to fix the 10 mistakes in the letter below. Look for spelling, capitalization, punctuation, and grammar mistakes.

9545 Bay View Lane

Dublin, Ohio

October 22, 2012

Dear Grandma and Grandpa,

I wanted to write to tell you about Buster. He's my new puppy! Busters fur is black, and his ears are pointed. Hes always sniffing around. He likes chasing ducks at the Pond. They get so mad at him! Buster wants to play all the time, and he loves being outside. Right now, dad is giving Buster a bath in tomato juice! Thats what we had to use becuz he surprized a skunk in our yard. Mom says the juice will take out the skunk smell. I sure hope so! Please write and tell me how your doing. I can barely weight for your visit here next month.

You're grandson,

Alex

5.W.2, 5.L.1, 5.L.2, 5.L.4

The Fox and the Crow

A crow found a piece of cheese on the ground. She quickly swooped down to pick up the food and perched on a limb to enjoy the tasty treat. A fox wandered by and saw this.

1. This is one of Aesop's fables. What is a fable?
   A. A funny story   B. A true story   C. A story that teaches a lesson

2. What does the title tell us about the characters? _____

3. Are the animals personified in the first paragraph? Explain. _____

4. What was the first thing the crow did after grabbing the cheese? _____
   _____

Day 1

"Good afternoon, Crow," the fox called out politely. "How lovely you look today! I bet your voice is just as beautiful and that you sing the sweetest of all of the birds in the forest."

1. What compliment did the fox pay the crow? _____

2. What does a crow sound like? _____

3. Why do you think the fox said nice things to the crow? _____

4. During what time of day does this fable take place? _____

Day 2

The crow began to feel proud as she listened to the fox. She puffed up her feathers, lifted her beak into the air, and opened her mouth to show the fox her musical voice. Just as she did this, the cheese fell out of her mouth and tumbled to the ground. The fox grabbed the cheese and hungrily devoured it.

1. Why did the crow drop the cheese? _____

2. Do you think the fox meant those compliments? Explain. _____

3. What was the first thing the fox did after grabbing the cheese? _____

4. What clues tell you that the fox was probably hungrier than the crow? _____
   _____

Day 3

The fox smiled slyly. As he walked away, he called back to the crow, "It is not wise to trust those who praise you with many compliments."

1. Restate the fox's message in your own words. _____

2. What was the fox's message?   A. Always share your cheese.
   B. Always compliment others.   C. Beware of false compliments.

3. Has anyone ever complimented you to get you to do something he wanted? If so, did it work? _____

4. Have you ever complimented someone to get what you wanted? If so, did it work? _____

Day 4

The Oak Tree and the Reeds

A mighty oak tree grew along a riverbank. Its trunk was thick, and its branches reached upward into the sky. It towered proudly above a patch of reeds that grew below it along the edge of the water.

On most days, a breeze blew across the river. The leaves of the mighty oak danced, but its branches held firmly in place. The oak laughed at the reeds because the wind was not so kind to them. The reeds trembled and shook as they struggled to stand up straight. But, the reeds did not mind the laughter of the oak; after all, the tree was so much bigger and stronger.

One day, a terrible hurricane approached the river. Its violent winds pulled up the roots of the mighty oak and tossed it to the ground. When the storm was over, the great tree lay in the patch of reeds.

The oak spoke sadly, "The strong winds were able to pick me up and throw me to the ground like a stick. Yet you reeds were able to stay rooted even though you are much smaller. How could this be?"

One reed spoke. "We may be small, but we know how to bend, whether the wind blows gently or violently. You, mighty oak, were too proud and did not know how to bend."

1. By reading the title, do you think this is one of Aesop's fables? _____

2. What types of objects are the two characters in this fable? _____
    _____

3. How is the oak tree different from the reeds? _____
    _____
    _____

4. What is the lesson of this fable?

    A. It can be better to be flexible than to be strong.

    B. It is OK to laugh at those smaller than you.

    C. Stay out of the way of a hurricane.

5. How might a nonfiction article describe the differences between an oak tree and
    reeds differently from this fable? _____
    _____
    _____
    _____

5.RL.1, 5.RL.2, 5.RL.3, 5.RL.7, 5.RL.9, 5.RL.10, 5.RF.4, 5.L.3, 5.L.4., 5.L.5

Prewrite/Brainstorm

When fiction writers select a narrator to tell the story, they choose a point of view. First-person narrators use I/me/my pronouns. Third-person narrators use he/she or the characters' names. On the lines below, list some things that might happen when you take your pet to the veterinarian.

_____

_____

_____

_____

Day 1

Draft

Write a short paragraph about taking a pet to the veterinarian. Write the paragraph using either first- or third-person narration.

_____

_____

_____

_____

Day 2

Revise

Revise your paragraph. Is the point of view clear? How does the reader know what the point of view is? Rewrite the paragraph, making sure that the point of view is clear.

_____

_____

_____

_____

Day 3

Proofread

Read your paragraph again. Do you see any capitalization errors? Are all of the words spelled correctly? Did you use the correct punctuation and grammar? Use proofreading marks to correct the sentences.

❏ Capitalization mistakes
❏ Grammar mistakes
❏ Punctuation mistakes
❏ Spelling mistakes

Day 4

Publish

Write your final copy on a computer or on the lines below.

MAKE SURE it turns out

- NEAT—Make sure there are no wrinkles, creases, or holes.
- CLEAN—Erase any smudges or dirty spots.
- EASY TO READ—Use your best handwriting and good spacing between words.

_____

_____

_____

_____

_____

_____

_____

_____

_____

_____

_____

_____

_____

_____

_____

_____

_____

_____

_____

_____

_____

_____

5.W.1, 5.W.2, 5.W.3, 5.W.4, 5.W.5, 5.W.6, 5.W.10, 5.L.2 CD-104600 • © Carson-Dellosa

Andrew, the Albatross

I love water sports, especially waterskiing. That's why I invited my best friend, Andrew, over to give it a try. Andrew had never been on waterskis before, but he was a good athlete. So, I thought waterskiing would be a **breeze** for him.

1. Who is Andrew? _____

2. What do you know about Andrew? _____

3. What does the word **breeze** mean in this sentence? _____

4. What clues suggest that waterskiing might not be a breeze for Andrew? _____
    _____

Day 1

Waterskiing is like flying to me. When I am being pulled on waterskis behind the boat, I feel like an eagle in flight. However, I realized Andrew was more of an albatross than an eagle.

1. How does the author feel about waterskiing? _____

2. What clues suggest the author is good at waterskiing? _____
    _____

3. Describe an eagle. _____

4. What is an albatross? _____

Day 2

On his first try, Andrew let go of the tow rope as soon as the boat started to move. He sank like an **anchor**. On his second try, he leaned into the skis, flipping head over heels like a gymnast.

1. What is an **anchor**? _____

2. Why is Andrew compared to an anchor? _____

3. What two similes does the author use to describe Andrew? _____
    _____

4. Write a simile for how you might look while waterskiing. _____

Day 3

On his third try, Andrew stood up. He teetered back and forth like a rag doll until he finally fell over. He held on to the rope long after he lost both skis. As he flopped at the end of the rope like a fish, I realized that waterskiing is not for everyone.

1. What two similes are used to describe Andrew? _____

2. What is your favorite simile from this week's reading? _____

3. Is the title of the passage a metaphor or a simile? _____

4. Write a metaphor that could be used to describe the author of the passage. ___
    _____

Day 4

Whitesox

Sanding the board,
My sweet Whitesox.

Her tongue,
Like fine grains of sand
On paper,
Licking the wood.

She is an electric sander,
Giving out a quiet purr.
She is a nail file,
Smoothing out the edges.

1. What is Whitesox? _____

2. Draw a picture of Whitesox in the box._

3. List the simile (comparison using **like** or **as**)._____

4. List the metaphors (comparison without using **like** or **as**). _____

_____

_____

 5.RL.1, 5.RL.2, 5.RL.3, 5.RL.4, 5.RL.5, 5.RL.6, 5.RL.10, 5.RF.4, 5.L.3, 5.L.5 CD-104600 • © Carson-Dellosa

Prewrite/Brainstorm

Poetry is different from prose writing. Prose writing appears in sentences and paragraphs. Poetry appears in lines and stanzas. Brainstorm about the five senses and create a list of sensory words that describe water.

Water

Sight	Smell	Hearing	Taste	Touch
_____	_____	_____	_____	_____
_____	_____	_____	_____	_____
_____	_____	_____	_____	_____

Day 1

Draft

Stanzas divide groups of lines and are like paragraphs. Take your ideas about water and write a poem in quatrains (four lines in each stanza). For longer poems, use another sheet of paper.

_____

_____

_____

_____

Day 2

Revise

Read the poem you wrote about water. Are the lines broken into quatrains? Do you want the lines to rhyme? Do the sensory words tell the reader what you think of water? Rewrite the poem, revising your words.

_____

_____

_____

_____

Day 3

Proofread

Read your poem again. Do you see any capitalization errors? Are all of the words spelled correctly? Did you use the correct punctuation and grammar? Use proofreading marks to correct the sentences.

- ❏ Capitalization mistakes
- ❏ Grammar mistakes
- ❏ Punctuation mistakes
- ❏ Spelling mistakes

Day 4

Publish

Write your final copy on a computer or on the lines below.
MAKE SURE it turns out

- NEAT—Make sure there are no wrinkles, creases, or holes.
- CLEAN—Erase any smudges or dirty spots.
- EASY TO READ—Use your best handwriting and good spacing between words.

_____

_____

_____

_____

_____

_____

_____

_____

_____

_____

_____

_____

_____

_____

_____

_____

_____

_____

_____

_____

A Delicious Dinner

Molly is Chinese American. Each week, her family members gather and serve a **traditional** Chinese meal. This week, Molly invited her friend Amy to join them for it.

1. Which word has an **e-consonant-e** to create the **long e** sound? _____

2. What does **traditional** mean?
   A. Customs handed down from one generation to another
   B. Really old-fashioned   C. Boring

3. What is the "it" in "join them for it"? _____

4. Is Molly from China? _____

Day 1

Molly's family was **busy** preparing for dinner when Amy arrived. Molly directed Amy through the living room to the kitchen, which was filled with many **good smells**. Molly and Amy set the table. They gave each person a pair of chopsticks, a soup bowl, a soup spoon, and a rice bowl on a saucer.

1. Which word rhymes with **busy: Susy** or **dizzy**? _____

2. Which word would best replace **good smells: aroma** or **odor**? _____

3. How many individual items do the girls set at each place? _____

4. How many chopsticks does each person get? _____

Day 2

The two girls went into the kitchen. Molly's father was slicing and chopping vegetables. He threw the vegetables into a large cooking pan coated with hot oil. "That's a wok," Molly said. Amy watched the vegetables sizzle.

1. Fill the blanks with homophones: After we cook dinner in the _____, we can go for a _____.

2. What is a wok? _____

3. Find an example of onomatopoeia. _____

4. How do you think Amy is used to eating? _____

Day 3

Molly's mother scooped different foods onto big plates. Amy carried steamed rice. It was one of the few dishes she recognized. There were meat-filled bundles called wontons, steamed noodles, stir-fried beef, sweet-and-sour chicken, and pork spareribs. The **nutritious** food was seasoned with herbs, spices, and sauces.

1. What sound does the **-tious** in **nutritious** make: **teeus** or **shus**? _____

2. What does **nutritious** mean? _____

3. Circle the name of the only thing Amy was familiar with before the dinner.
   wok   chopsticks   rice   wontons

4. Do you think Amy was upset about being asked to help? _____

Day 4

A Delicious Dinner (continued)

Once everyone was at the table, they quickly began eating. Their chopsticks moved quickly and made small clicking noises as they grabbed the food.

Amy was a little nervous about eating with chopsticks. Molly gave her instructions on how to hold and pinch with the chopsticks.

Amy finally managed to pick up a piece of chicken with her chopsticks. Suddenly, her fingers slipped, and the chicken flew across the table. It landed in Molly's soup with a *splash*. Everyone smiled. Molly's grandmother, who came every week to the family meal, patted Amy on the arm.

"We keep these on hand for visitors," she said kindly. She brought out a fork and knife and handed them to Amy.

Amy was relieved. She ate the rest of her dinner easily. It was delicious!

At the end of the meal, everyone was given a fortune cookie. Amy broke hers open and read it. "If you practice hard, you will learn many things." Amy laughed and said, "If you let me take home a pair of chopsticks, my fortune may come true!"

1. Write a compound word from the story. _____

2. Which meaning of fortune is used here: lots of money or a prediction? _____
   _____

3. Write two examples of onomatopoeia from the story. _____
   _____

4. What did Molly's grandmother do to make Amy feel comfortable?_____
   _____

5. Write a different ending for the story. _____
   _____
   _____
   _____

5.RL.1, 5.RL.2, 5.RL.3, 5.RL.4, 5.RL.10, 5.RF.3, 5.RF.4, 5.L.4, 5.L.5   CD-104600 • © Carson-Dellosa

Name_____

Prewrite/Brainstorm

Use a story map to plan a story about a new student beginning fifth grade.

1. A. Setting: _____ B. Characters: _____

   C. Problem: _____

2. First event: _____

3. Second event: _____

4. Third event: _____

5. Resolution: _____

Day 1

Draft

Begin your narrative by writing an introduction paragraph. Set the stage for your story by describing the characters, the setting, and the problem. Include the problem and an interesting opening sentence that will make your reader want to keep reading.

_____

_____

_____

_____

Day 2

Revise

Revise your paragraph. Read your first draft. Can you be more specific? Do you have information that you do not need? Do you want to change your sentence order? Rewrite your ideas in a new paragraph.

_____

_____

_____

_____

Day 3

Proofread

Read your paragraph again. Do you see any capitalization errors? Are all of the words spelled correctly? Did you use the correct punctuation and grammar? Use proofreading marks to correct the sentences.

- ❑ Capitalization mistakes
- ❑ Grammar mistakes
- ❑ Punctuation mistakes
- ❑ Spelling mistakes

Day 4

Publish

Write your final copy on a computer or on the lines below.
MAKE SURE it turns out

- NEAT—Make sure there are no wrinkles, creases, or holes.
- CLEAN—Erase any smudges or dirty spots.
- EASY TO READ—Use your best handwriting and good spacing between words.

_____

_____

_____

_____

_____

_____

_____

_____

_____

_____

_____

_____

_____

_____

_____

_____

_____

_____

_____

_____

The Understudy

It was almost time for the play to begin, but the lead actress had not arrived. When the door opened, everyone looked up, expecting to see Beth.

1. What clues does the title give you about what will happen in this passage? _____

   _____

2. Who was the lead actress? _____

3. What problem is introduced in the paragraph? _____

4. What do you think will happen next? _____

Day 1

"I hate to put a damper on things, but Beth has a fever and will not make it tonight," explained her mom.

"Well, I never put all of my eggs in one basket," responded Ms. King. "Amanda has been our understudy for that part and knows it well. Amanda, put on Beth's costume."

1. An idiom is an expression that means something different from what it actually says. List any idioms in this selection. _____

2. How did Ms. King respond to the problem? _____

3. Had Amanda worked hard as the understudy? _____

4. What clues from the paragraph helped you answer question 3? _____

Day 2

Amanda was on cloud nine after the performance. She greeted her family who were waiting at the back of the auditorium.

"You were terrific. You are the apple of my eye," said Dad, as he gave Amanda a hug. Amanda was speechless as everyone complimented her.

1. List any idioms in this selection. _____

2. Was Amanda pleased with her performance? How do you know? _____

3. Why do you think Amanda was speechless after the performance? _____

4. How would you have reacted in Amanda's position? _____

Day 3

Dad said, "It's raining cats and dogs outside. Grandpa, keep an eye on everyone while I run and get the car."

Finally, Dad returned. "Sorry it took so long. The traffic is slower than molasses in January. I avoided an accident by the skin of my teeth."

1. What members of Amanda's family were at the performance? _____

2. List any idioms in this selection. _____

3. Replace one of the idioms with another idiom. _____

4. What could someone learn from this story? _____

Day 4

I Should Have Bitten My Tongue

My friends and I were having a good time when, out of the blue, Jayla asked me about my trip to Jamaica. I wanted to fly the coop! A couple of days before, I had lied about going to Jamaica. Jayla is always bragging about her fantastic vacations. For once, I wanted to hold a candle to her, but now I was caught with my foot in my mouth.

"What's wrong? Cat got your tongue?" Jayla teased. She smiled roguishly at me. She knew she had me over a barrel.

I asked her to drop it, but she had a one-track mind. I was a sitting duck to her verbal jabs. Then, she started bragging about all of her trips around the world. Everyone was all ears. If you ask me, Jayla is too big for her britches!

1. An idiom is an expression that means something different from what it actually says. Underline all of the idioms in this selection.

2. Match the idioms in paragraph 1 with the literal meaning below.

   A. Be compared equally to _____

   B. Without warning _____

   C. Escape _____

   D. Having said something you wish you could take back _____

3. Write a literal meaning for one of the idioms in paragraph 2. _____

   _____

4. What is the bigger problem in this selection—the lie or the bragging? Explain. _____

   _____

   _____

   _____

   _____

Prewrite/Brainstorm

Continue writing the narrative you started on week 8. Look back at the first two events on your story map. List descriptive words about the first and second events.

First and second events:

_____ _____ _____

_____ _____ _____

_____ _____ _____

Draft

Now, draft a paragraph describing the first and second events that happened when a new student began fifth grade. Use the ideas you wrote on your brainstorming list.

_____

_____

_____

_____

Revise

Revise your paragraphs about the new student. Read your first draft. Can you be more specific? Do you have information that you do not need? Do you want to change your sentence order? Rewrite your paragraph.

_____

_____

_____

_____

Proofread

Read your paragraphs again. Do you see any capitalization errors? Are all of the words spelled correctly? Did you use the correct punctuation and grammar? Use proofreading marks to correct the sentences.

- ❏ Capitalization mistakes
- ❏ Grammar mistakes
- ❏ Punctuation mistakes
- ❏ Spelling mistakes

Publish

Write your final copy on a computer or on the lines below.

MAKE SURE it turns out

- NEAT—Make sure there are no wrinkles, creases, or holes.
- CLEAN—Erase any smudges or dirty spots.
- EASY TO READ—Use your best handwriting and good spacing between words.

_____

_____

_____

_____

_____

_____

_____

_____

_____

_____

_____

_____

_____

_____

_____

_____

_____

_____

_____

_____

_____

Where, Oh Where?

I'm a very **forgetful** person, so it didn't surprise any of my friends when I shouted, "I've lost my science report!"

1. Which part of **forgetful** is the root, and which part is the suffix? _____

2. What does **forgetful** mean? _____

3. If you were reading this story aloud, describe how you would read, "I've lost my science report!" _____

4. Which point of view is this written from?
    A. First person   B. Second person   C. Third person

Day 1

Paul, Adam, and Leo all gave **suggestions** as to possible locations of the report, but one by one, they were eliminated. I hadn't stopped at my locker, the girls' gym, the computer lab, or the cafeteria. I even called home, to see if I had left it there.

1. Which **gg** or **g** sounds like the **gg** in **suggestions**: **giggle** or **gingerbread**? _____

2. What does **eliminated** mean in this paragraph? _____

3. The author's friends tried to help. What would you have done in this situation?

    _____

4. What clues suggest whether the author is a boy or a girl? _____

    _____

Day 2

Mom was particularly upset, especially because she had been the one driving me all over town while I was doing research and buying just the right shade of light blue printer paper. She had also done me the huge favor of typing the 10-page report.

"Tara! How could you possibly **misplace** something so important? Did you check your backpack? Your locker?" Then, she repeated my friends' suggestions.

1. Which word in this paragraph is a synonym for **lose**? _____

2. Divide the word **misplace** into its syllables. _____

3. How would you read aloud the mother's words? _____

4. What new information do you learn about the author? _____

Day 3

I had one period left before science, and I was pretty nervous. I needed another A in science so that I would have straight A's across the sheet. This report was a major part of our final grade in Mrs. Hernandez's class. As I sat in **geography**, mentally retracing my steps and combing my memory for ideas on the report's location, I had a great idea.

1. Which word uses the same consonant twice, each pronounced differently? _____

2. The word **geography** came from **geo**, which means "earth," and **graphein**, which means "to write." So, what does the word **geography** mean? _____

3. Will Tara remember anything the teacher said in her geography class? _____

4. How well does Tara normally do in school? How do you know? _____

Day 4

Where, Oh Where? (continued)

I decided that I would tell Mrs. Hernandez that I would do further research because I was so excited about the subject and that I hadn't finished typing it. I would tell her that my mother had offered to finish typing it but had broken her finger. I would come up with some incredible and airtight excuse.

As I slowly wandered toward the science lab, silently rehearsing my excuses, I began to feel **guilty**. Could I actually look my favorite teacher in the eye and lie about my report? How would I feel then? Maybe I would feel worse than I felt when I realized that it was missing.

I tossed my backpack over my shoulder, straightened my back, and walked into the room. Taking a deep breath, I knew what I had to do—I would tell the truth.

I walked up to Mrs. Hernandez's desk to speak with her. As she looked up from the thick stack of papers in front of her, she lightly tapped the top report, a report typed on baby-blue paper in a transparent folder.

"Oh, Tara!" said Mrs. Hernandez. "I'm always glad when one or two students hand in these larger reports early. I can really take my time reading them then. Your research on whale migration is incredible. Would you mind sharing with the class?"

I thought I would fall over! How in the world had this happened?

1. Is the **ui** sound in **guilty** more like the **ui** sound in **suite** or **build**? _____

    _____

2. What does **guilty** mean? _____

    _____

3. If you were reading this story aloud, what facial expression would you use for Tara's response to her teacher's words? _____

    _____

4. Does the teacher sound pleased with Tara's report? How do you know? _____

    _____

    _____

5. What had Tara really forgotten? _____

    _____

Prewrite/Brainstorm

It is time to write about the third event in the narrative you worked on in Weeks 8 and 10. Look back at what you wrote for that event on your story map. Take that idea and make a list of descriptive words about the third event.

Third event:

_____   _____   _____

_____   _____   _____

_____   _____   _____

Day 1

Draft

Conclude your narrative by drafting a paragraph that wraps up everything that happened when a new student began fifth grade. Use the ideas you wrote on your brainstorming list. Be sure to include the resolution to the story problem.

_____

_____

_____

_____

Day 2

Revise

Revise your paragraphs about the new student. Read your first draft. Can you be more specific? Do you have information that you do not need? Do you want to change your sentence order? Rewrite your paragraph. Change nouns, verbs, and adjectives to more specific words and use complete sentences.

_____

_____

_____

_____

Day 3

Proofread

Read your paragraphs again. Do you see any capitalization errors? Are all of the words spelled correctly? Did you use the correct punctuation and grammar? Use proofreading marks to correct the sentences.

- ❏ Capitalization mistakes
- ❏ Grammar mistakes
- ❏ Punctuation mistakes
- ❏ Spelling mistakes

Day 4

Publish

Write your final copy on a computer or on the lines below.

MAKE SURE it turns out

- NEAT—Make sure there are no wrinkles, creases, or holes.
- CLEAN—Erase any smudges or dirty spots.
- EASY TO READ—Use your best handwriting and good spacing between words.

_____

_____

_____

_____

_____

_____

_____

_____

_____

_____

_____

_____

_____

_____

_____

_____

_____

_____

_____

Australian Animals

Australia's animals are unique. They include marsupials and monotremes. Both are mammals. Marsupials carry their babies in pouches. Monotremes give birth to their young by laying eggs. However, they produce milk to feed their babies.

1. What is the subject of this passage? _____

2. Is the passage fiction or nonfiction? _____

3. What makes monotremes unique? _____

4. What makes marsupials unique? _____

Day 1

The **Tasmanian** devil is a ferocious marsupial that lives on the island of Tasmania. It has black fur and very sharp teeth. It eats other mammals, birds, and reptiles.

1. What kind of animal is the Tasmanian devil? _____

2. How did the **Tasmanian** part of its name come about? _____

3. Is the Tasmanian devil a carnivore or an herbivore? _____

4. Draw a picture of a Tasmanian devil on another sheet of paper.

Day 2

Because the duck-billed platypus hatches its young from eggs, it is a monotreme. It has soft fur, a snout, webbed feet and claws, and a flat tail like a beaver. It lives near rivers and creeks, where it eats crawfish, worms, and small fish.

1. What kind of animal is the duck-billed platypus? _____

2. What animal is the duck-billed platypus compared to? _____

3. List other animals that share one characteristic with the duck-billed platypus.
   _____

4. Draw a picture of a duck-billed platypus on another sheet of paper.

Day 3

Kangaroos are marsupials. Baby kangaroos, called joeys, live in their mother's pouches for five to six months. Kangaroos can hop at about 40 miles per hour (about 64.3 kph). They have strong hind legs for leaping about 30 to 40 feet (about 9 to 12 m). Kangaroos are herbivores.

1. What does an herbivore eat?
   A. Meat   B. Plants   C. Metal

2. What kind of animal is a kangaroo? _____

3. How does a kangaroo get around? _____

4. Draw a picture of a kangaroo on another sheet of paper.

Day 4

Australia and the United States: Alike or Different?

How are Australia and the United States alike? How are they different? Australia is in the Southern Hemisphere. The United States is in the Northern Hemisphere. Australia's summer months are December through February, which are the United States' winter months. Summer months in the United States are June through August, which are Australia's winter months. In the Northern Hemisphere, hurricanes and tornadoes spin in a clockwise direction. In the Southern Hemisphere, they spin in a counterclockwise direction.

Australians drive on the left side of the road, while people in the United States drive on the right side of the road. Australia's population is about 19 million. That's about the same as the total of the six most populated cities in the United States. Australia has kangaroos, anteaters, emus, and koalas, but in the United States, you'll find those animals only in zoos.

The official head of Australia's government is the queen of England. In the United States, it is the president. Australians elect people to a legislature, and a prime minister is the functional head of government. Australia has three major political parties, whereas the United States has only two. An Australian law says that people who are able to vote must vote. If not, they can be fined. The United States has no such law.

1. What does the title tell us the passage will be about? _____

2. Complete the Venn diagram using information from the passage.

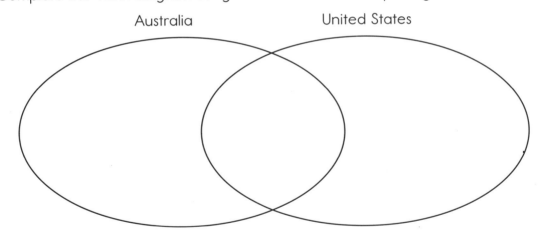

Australia   United States

3. What do you think is the most interesting difference between Australia and the United States? _____

_____

_____

Name_____

Prewrite/Brainstorm

Writing to compare is interesting and effective. Think of your favorite fruit and favorite vegetable. Use the Venn diagram to compare them.

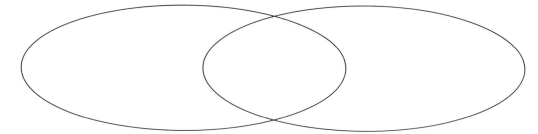

Draft

When you look at your Venn diagram, you will want to focus on similarities and differences. Write a paragraph to compare the fruit and the vegetable.

_____

_____

_____

_____

Revise

Look at your paragraph. Do all of the sentences talk about the same idea? What information could you add? What sentences would you change? Write your changes.

_____

_____

_____

_____

Proofread

Read your paragraph again. Do you see any capitalization errors? Are all of the words spelled correctly? Did you use the correct punctuation and grammar? Use proofreading marks to correct the sentences.

❐ Capitalization mistakes
❐ Grammar mistakes
❐ Punctuation mistakes
❐ Spelling mistakes

Publish

Write your final copy on a computer or on the lines below.
MAKE SURE it turns out
- NEAT—Make sure there are no wrinkles, creases, or holes.
- CLEAN—Erase any smudges or dirty spots.
- EASY TO READ—Use your best handwriting and good spacing between words.

_____

_____

_____

_____

_____

_____

_____

_____

_____

_____

_____

_____

_____

_____

_____

_____

_____

_____

_____

_____

_____

_____

The Sydney Opera House

The Sydney Opera House is world famous. It has an unusual design. It is one of the most unusual buildings in the world. The opera house is Sydney's most famous landmark. It is located in Sydney Harbor.

1. What clues does the title give you about the passage? _____

2. Does the first paragraph tell you where Sydney is? _____

3. Do you think the opera house is near water? _____

4. What details from the paragraph helped you answer question 3? _____

   _____

Day 1

Danish architect Jørn Utzon designed the Sydney Opera House. He won a contest for his design. Work began in 1959 and was completed in 1973. The estimate for the Sydney Opera House was $7 million (Australian). However, the final cost was $102 million.

1. Does this paragraph give you a clue about where Sydney is? If so, where? _____

   _____

2. How long did it take to build the Sydney Opera House? _____

3. How much was the building estimated to cost? _____

4. Was the cost estimate accurate? Explain. _____

Day 2

Utzon wanted the roof to look like sails on a giant sailing ship. Some people think the roof looks like huge seashells. The roof is made of 10 gigantic arched-concrete shell shapes. The shells have ribs that curve inward. Concrete joins the ribs where they meet. One of the biggest cranes in the world lifted the concrete roof pieces into place. Working on the building was dangerous because of the roof.

1. Does the Sydney Opera House look like Utzon wanted it to? _____

2. What clues helped you answer question 1? _____

3. What holds the ribs of the shells in place? _____

4. What do you think the danger was with the roof? _____

Day 3

The opera house contains one hall for operas. The orchestra plays in another hall. A third hall is for plays. A fourth is for chamber music. The fifth is for exhibitions.

1. What fraction of halls are used for music? _____

2. What kind of music do orchestras and chamber music groups play?
   A. Hip-hop   B. Classical   C. Contemporary country

3. Which, if any, of the activities that take place in the Sydney Opera House would you enjoy? Explain. _____

4. What kind of music or other event do you think they should have at the opera house? _____

Day 4

Lighthouses

Imagine you're trying to get home. A storm has been raging for hours. The sea has been tossing your small sailing craft up and down, and you are not sure where you are. Suddenly in the distance, you see a faint light. You know you are safe and almost home.

Lighthouses were built to guide ships into coastal waters. They were built at dangerous points on coastlines, usually near reefs or at entrances to harbors. The earliest known lighthouse was built in Egypt. It was called Pharos. Pharos was completed about 280 BC.

Boston Light was built in 1716. It was the first lighthouse in the colonies. By the time the Declaration of Independence was signed in 1776, the United States had 12 lighthouses, mostly in New England. In 1800, the United States had 16 lighthouses, and by 1812, it had about 49 lighthouses. The first West Coast lighthouses were completed in 1854 and 1855 in California.

1. Is this passage fiction or nonfiction? _____

2. How does the author hook the reader? _____

3. Why were lighthouses built? _____

4. Why do you think so many lighthouses were built during the colonial days? _____

_____

_____

5. Research a lighthouse. Draw an illustration in the box above to show your findings. Write a caption for your illustration.

5.RI.1, 5.RI.2, 5.RI.3, 5.RI.4, 5.RI.5, 5.RI.6, 5.RI.7, 5.RI.8, 5.RI.9, 5.RI.10, 5.RF.4, 5.L.3 CD-104600 • © Carson-Dellosa

Prewrite/Brainstorm

Realistic fiction is a story that could be true but is not. It has two main purposes: to tell an interesting story and to send an important message (theme). Use the graphic organizer to write a realistic fiction story. Read the information and then fill in the boxes with your ideas.

Setting: _____   Main Characters: _____

Theme: _____

Problem: _____

Event 1: _____

Event 2: _____

Event 3: _____

Solution: _____

Day 1

Draft

Write your realistic fiction story. Follow the graphic organizer you made to help you describe the problem, the three events, and the solution.

_____
_____
_____
_____

Day 2

Revise

Read your realistic fiction story. How could you improve it? Do you need to add more details? Do you need to rearrange the order of events? Rewrite your story.

_____
_____
_____
_____

Day 3

Proofread

Read your story again. Do you see any capitalization errors? Are all of the words spelled correctly? Did you use the correct punctuation and grammar? Use proofreading marks to correct the sentences.

❐ Capitalization mistakes
❐ Grammar mistakes
❐ Punctuation mistakes
❐ Spelling mistakes

Day 4

Publish

Write your final copy on a computer or on the lines below.
MAKE SURE it turns out

- NEAT—Make sure there are no wrinkles, creases, or holes.
- CLEAN—Erase any smudges or dirty spots.
- EASY TO READ—Use your best handwriting and good spacing between words.

_____

_____

_____

_____

_____

_____

_____

_____

_____

_____

_____

_____

_____

_____

_____

_____

_____

_____

_____

_____

5.W.3, 5.W.4, 5.W.5, 5.W.6, 5.W.10, 5.L.1, 5.L.2

Green plants are like factories. Plant factories make two kinds of food: One is sugar, and the other is starch. Almost all fruits and vegetables you eat contain some form of sugar or starch. Fruits such as apples, oranges, cherries, pears, and even lemons contain sugar; vegetables such as potatoes, corn, and beans contain starch.

1. Circle words with a **soft g** sound and underline words with a **hard g** sound.

2. What does the author compare green plants with? _____

3. What is a factory? _____

4. What two kinds of food do plant factories make? _____

   _____

Day 1

Green plants are made up of cells just as you are. A cell is the smallest structural unit of a living plant or animal. Because they are so small, cells can be seen only through a microscope. Inside the cells are chloroplasts, which contain chlorophyll and carotene. They manufacture the sugar and starch. They are the machines of the plant factory.

1. List the words that begin with the same starting sound as **clean**. _____

   _____

2. What is a microscope? _____

3. What is compared to the machines of a factory? _____

4. Can you see cells with the naked eye? _____

Day 2

Two kinds of doors are in plant factories. One kind is called stoma. Stomata are tiny holes in leaves that allow air to move in and out. Plants use carbon dioxide and then release oxygen back into the air. Roots are the second kind of door. Water travels into the root hairs of the plant.

1. Circle the words with **oo** that sound like **boots**. Underline the words with **oo** that sound like **floor**.

2. What are stomata? _____

3. What is a good title for this paragraph? _____

4. What are the two kinds of doors in plant factories? _____

Day 3

Plants use storerooms to **store** their food. Carrot plants store their food in roots, while maple trees store their food in trunks. Lettuce plants store their food in leaves, peas store their food in seeds, and peach trees store their food in the fruit.

1. Find and circle a compound word.

2. What word could you use instead of **store** as it is used in this paragraph?_____

3. Underline the topic sentence of this paragraph.

4. Draw lines to match the plants to their storerooms.

carrot	fruit
lettuce	root
peas	trunk
peach tree	seeds
maple tree	leaves

Day 4

Your Brain

Have you ever watched a coach during a ball game? The coach tells players where to go and what to do as things are happening in the game. Your brain is like your coach. Information from your five senses—touch, smell, hearing, taste, sight—races to your brain. Your brain sorts out the information and lets your body know what to do.

Your brain has three main parts: the medulla oblongata, the cerebrum, and the cerebellum. Perhaps you have heard someone talk about "gray matter" while discussing intelligence. This refers to the cerebrum. The cerebrum is large, and its outside layer, called the cerebral cortex, is gray and looks wrinkled. The cerebrum and the cerebral cortex spring to work when you are doing something that requires a good deal of thought. If you are taking a test, talking to a friend, or reading directions to put together a new bike, your cerebrum is busy.

As you try to keep your balance on your bike, it is your cerebellum that is called to work. The cerebellum is in control of balance and coordination. It is much smaller than the cerebrum.

The medulla oblongata is your brain stem. It is the lowest part of your brain. The medulla oblongata controls breathing and heart rate.

The next time you assemble a bike, take a bike ride, and gasp for breath after riding up a hill, you will know that all of the parts of your brain have been very busy.

1. What is the main idea of this passage? _____
   _____
   _____

2. How are the supporting paragraphs organized? _____
   _____

3. How is a brain like a coach? _____
   _____
   _____

4. Label the three main parts of the brain.

Prewrite/Brainstorm

Choose a topic to write a report about. Use a KWL chart to organize what you know and what you want to know. Then, research what you want to know and complete the third column.

I **K**now	I **W**ant to Know	I **L**earned

Draft

Using the information from your KWL chart, write your report. Draft your opening paragraph. Your opening paragraph should give general information about your topic and provide the reader with information about what he will learn. Continue writing the rest of your report on the computer or on another sheet of paper.

_____

_____

_____

_____

Revise

Read your report. Did you begin each paragraph with a sentence that introduces the topic of the paragraph? Did you write at least three supporting sentences about the topic? Revise your first paragraph on the lines below. Then, continue revising your report on the computer or on the paper draft of your report.

_____

_____

_____

_____

Proofread

Read your report again. Do you see any capitalization errors? Are all of the words spelled correctly? Did you use the correct punctuation and grammar? Use proofreading marks to correct the sentences.

- ❐ Capitalization mistakes
- ❐ Grammar mistakes
- ❐ Punctuation mistakes
- ❐ Spelling mistakes

Publish

Write your final copy on a computer or on the lines below.
MAKE SURE it turns out

- NEAT—Make sure there are no wrinkles, creases, or holes.
- CLEAN—Erase any smudges or dirty spots.
- EASY TO READ—Use your best handwriting and good spacing between words.

_____

_____

_____

_____

_____

_____

_____

_____

_____

_____

_____

_____

_____

_____

_____

_____

_____

_____

_____

_____

Television

Television gave people a window to see other people, places, and events around the world. More than 98 percent of all US homes have a television. Television is now an **important** form of communication, allowing people instant access to current events.

1. What clue does the title give you about the topic of this passage? _____

2. Does the first paragraph narrow down the topic? If so, how? _____

3. Rewrite the last sentence, using a synonym for **important**. _____

4. What is the topic sentence of this paragraph? _____

Day 1

Television does not have just one inventor. In the 1800s, an Italian inventor named Guglielmo Marconi set the stage when he discovered how to send signals through the air as electromagnetic waves. His invention was the radio. In the early 1900s, a young American named Philo Farnsworth had an idea to send pictures as well as sound through the air. This led to the invention of the electronic television camera.

1. What other invention set the stage for the invention of the television? _____

2. About how many years passed between the two inventions? _____

3. What was the next step? _____

4. About how many years have passed between that invention and now? _____

Day 2

At about the same time, an American scientist named Vladimir Zworykin invented the iconoscope and the kinescope. The iconoscope was a television camera. The kinescope was a picture tube to receive and show the picture. In 1929, Zworykin made the first television system.

1. What were the next steps in the invention of television? _____

2. Inventors from which country were involved in the most steps? _____

3. Do you know anyone who was alive in 1929? _____

4. Do you think Farnsworth or Zworykin made a lot of money from their invention of the television? _____

Day 3

How does a television work? First, light and sound waves are changed into electronic signals by cameras and microphones. Next, these electronic signals are passed through the air and received by individual television sets. Last, the television set unscrambles the signals.

1. How many steps are there to get to the picture you see on your television? _____

2. What are those steps? _____

_____

3. Which kinds of waves are changed into electronic signals? _____

4. What is the most important thing about television for you? _____

Day 4

Philo Farnsworth and Television

What would you say if someone asked you who invented the television? If you do not know the answer, you are not alone. Most people do not know that Philo Farnsworth is credited with inventing the modern television.

Farnsworth was born in a log cabin in 1906. When he was 12, his family moved to a ranch. This put Farnsworth miles away from his school, so he rode his horse to get there.

Farnsworth was very curious about electrons and electricity. He asked one of his teachers to tutor him outside of class and to let him sit in on a course for older students. The teacher agreed. When Farnsworth was only 14, he came up with the idea of sending television pictures without using moving parts.

How did this invention work? Moving images, or pictures, were broken into pinpoints of light. These pinpoints were changed into electrical impulses, or movements. Then, the impulses were collected in the television set and changed back to light. People could then see the images.

When he died in 1971, Farnsworth held more than 300 patents for his inventions. A major magazine listed Farnsworth as one of the 100 greatest scientists and thinkers of the twentieth century. In addition, in 1983 the US Postal Service issued a stamp in his honor.

1. What is the main idea of this passage? _____

   _____

2. What is the main topic of paragraph 2? _____

   _____

3. What is the main topic of paragraph 3? _____

   _____

4. What is the main topic of paragraph 4? _____

   _____

5. What is the main topic of paragraph 5? _____

   _____

Prewrite/Brainstorm

A movie review gives the writer's opinion of a movie. Think about a movie you have seen recently. How would you rate it? Brainstorm and make a list of your opinions about the movie. What did or didn't you like? Would you recommend it? Think about who you are writing this review for.

_____

_____

_____

Day 1

Draft

Write a movie review that describes your opinion of the movie. Be sure to include a topic sentence that states the movie's name and explains your opinion. Conclude your review with your recommendation. Keep in mind who your audience is.

_____

_____

_____

_____

Day 2

Revise

Read your movie review. Does the review begin in an interesting way? Will the reader understand what the movie is about? Is your opinion of the movie clear? Will your review attract your audience? Rewrite the review with more specific words.

_____

_____

_____

_____

Day 3

Proofread

Read your movie review again. Do you see any capitalization errors? Are all of the words spelled correctly? Did you use the correct punctuation and grammar? Use proofreading marks to correct the sentences.

- ❏ Capitalization mistakes
- ❏ Grammar mistakes
- ❏ Punctuation mistakes
- ❏ Spelling mistakes

Day 4

Publish

Write your final copy on a computer or on the lines below.

MAKE SURE it turns out

- NEAT—Make sure there are no wrinkles, creases, or holes.
- CLEAN—Erase any smudges or dirty spots.
- EASY TO READ—Use your best handwriting and good spacing between words.

5.W.1, 5.W.4, 5.W.5, 5.W.6, 5.W.10, 5.L.1, 5.L.2

Name_____

Hooray for Hair

Have you ever considered the many characteristics of your hair? While your hair may improve your **appearance**, it also has important functions.

1. Does the **pear** in **appearance** sound more like **peer** or **pear**? _____

2. What does the title tell you about how the author feels about hair? _____
   _____

3. How does the author "hook" the reader? _____

4. Do you think this passage will provide solutions for bad hair days or information about hair? _____

Day 1

Hair protects the body. It acts as a cushion, protecting the head from bumps and bruises. Hair can be a shield from the hot summer sun and keep the head warm on chilly winter days. Inside the nose and ears, tiny hairs **deter** dirt, dust, and insects from entering the body. Eyebrows are patches of hair that trap **perspiration** before it is able to reach the eyes. Eyelashes prevent dirt and dust from infecting the eyes.

1. Which syllable do you emphasize when you say **deter**? _____

2. List the words that mean **keep away**. _____

3. What is another word for **perspiration**? _____

4. What hair protects our eyes? _____

Day 2

Each hair on the body grows from a root beneath the skin. This root forms a tiny tube called a **follicle**. As new hair cells grow from the root, the old cells are pushed up, and because they are no longer being fed, they soon die. The dead cells harden, forming a stack on top of a root, referred to as a hair shaft. Only the follicle and the root remain alive, so it does not hurt to cut hair.

1. What syllable do you emphasize when you say **follicle**? _____

2. What is a follicle? _____

3. What is a hair shaft made of? _____

4. What are the three parts of each hair? _____

Day 3

The shape of the hair shaft, as seen under a microscope, determines the degree of curliness or straightness. Straight hairs are round in structure. The flatter the hair shaft, the curlier the hair will be. You cannot change your hair follicles, but hair straighteners and permanents can alter the appearance of hair temporarily.

1. Have you ever wished for different hair? Explain. _____

2. What shape is your hair shaft? _____

3. Which two words in this paragraph are synonyms for **modify**? _____

4. What was the author's purpose in writing this pasage? _____
   _____

Day 4

The Right Choice

Throughout history, people have been faced with critical choices. Sometimes, people's choices have made the world a better place for everyone. Sometimes, they have made the world a better place only for themselves. It all comes down to choices.

The period of slavery in this country was a time of crucial choices. While some bound slaves in chains, others did all they could to oppose slavery. William Still, a free black man in Philadelphia, jeopardized his own safety and freedom to get others through the Underground Railroad route.

Despite the bounty on Harriet Tubman, she chose to keep helping others. She dressed up as a man and continued to help others escape. Harriet's friend, Thomas Garrett, a white businessman, was fined $5,400 (a huge amount in the 1800s) and arrested for his part in the Underground Railroad. Knowing he was doing the right thing, Thomas nevertheless continued his Underground Railroad work.

Fewer than 100 years later, society was once again faced with pivotal choices. There were those who chose to do the work of the Nazis by killing and imprisoning innocent Jewish people. Then, there was Miep Gies, the Dutch woman who helped hide Anne Frank's Jewish family for 25 months. There was Oskar Schindler, a German businessman. He saved more than 1,000 Polish Jewish people by having them work in his factory. The factory was actually a safe haven.

Today, people are still faced with choices about how to treat others. What choice will you make?

1. Write the adjectives the author uses to describe choices. _____

_____

2. What is the author's purpose in writing this passage? Circle all that apply.

   A. to inform the reader about people who have made the right choices

   B. to entertain the reader with the choices people have made

   C. to persuade the reader to make the right choices

   D. to persuade the reader to travel around the world to fight for injustice

3. Name a group of people who are discriminated against today. _____

_____

4. What choice will you make for or against this group? _____

_____

 5.RI.1, 5.RI.2, 5.RI.3, 5.RI.4, 5.RI.5, 5.RI.6, 5.RI.7, 5.RI.8, 5.RI.9, 5.RI.10, 5.RF.3, 5.RF.4, 5.L.4, 5.L.5 CD-104600 • © Carson-Dellosa

Prewrite/Brainstorm

Authors have a reason for writing: They want to entertain, inform, or persuade the reader. In persuasion, the writer wants to persuade the reader to do something or think a certain way. Begin to create a persuasive paragraph. First, list the reasons you think your parent should take you to the library.

_____

_____

_____

Day 1

Draft

Using your list of reasons to go to the library, draft a paragraph to persuade your parent to take you to the library. Remember to include a topic sentence and a concluding sentence.

_____

_____

_____

_____

Day 2

Revise

Look at your rough draft. Is it persuasive? Does it have a topic sentence? Does it have points that fit your topic sentence? Did you write a concluding sentence? Rewrite your paragraph, and make your words more specific.

_____

_____

_____

_____

Day 3

Proofread

Read your paragraph again. Do you see any capitalization errors? Are all of the words spelled correctly? Did you use the correct punctuation and grammar? Use proofreading marks to correct the sentences.

❒ Capitalization mistakes
❒ Grammar mistakes
❒ Punctuation mistakes
❒ Spelling mistakes

Day 4

Publish

Write your final copy on a computer or on the lines below.
MAKE SURE it turns out
- NEAT—Make sure there are no wrinkles, creases, or holes.
- CLEAN—Erase any smudges or dirty spots.
- EASY TO READ—Use your best handwriting and good spacing between words.

_____

_____

_____

_____

_____

_____

_____

_____

_____

_____

_____

_____

_____

_____

_____

_____

_____

_____

_____

_____

_____

_____

5.W.1, 5.W.4, 5.W.5, 5.W.6, 5.W.10, 5.L.1, 5.L.2, 5.L.3

Clara Brown was born a slave. In 1835, she and her family were **auctioned** off to different owners. Clara was sold to George Brown. Her husband and son were bought by slave traders. Her daughter Eliza was sold to another slave owner. Clara lost touch with all of her family.

1. Who is this passage about? _____

2. Is this article fiction or nonfiction? _____

3. What sound does the **ti** in **auctioned** make? _____

4. How is your life similar or different from Clara Brown's life? _____
   _____

Day 1

The 1850 census showed that about 4 million African Americans were living in the United States. Only 400,000 of these African Americans were free. Free African Americans had to obey laws established for them. They were not allowed to socialize with slaves. They also could not hold meetings.

1. What is the main idea of this paragraph? _____

2. What word has the **s** sound at the beginning, middle, and end? _____

3. Why were free African Americans not able to socialize with slaves? _____

4. Why did the author include this paragraph in a biography about Clara Brown?
   _____

Day 2

Clara became free in 1857. African Americans had to carry freedom papers at all times to prove that they were not runaway slaves. Clara took a job as a cook on a wagon train heading to Colorado. She hoped she would find her daughter Eliza there.

1. What is the root of the word **freedom**? _____

2. Why did free African Americans have to carry freedom papers? _____
   _____

3. Why did Clara take a job as a cook on a wagon train? _____

4. Why did she decide to go to Colorado? _____

Day 3

In Colorado, Clara started a laundry business. She charged 50 cents a shirt. She did very well with her business. She helped pay for ex-slaves to move to Colorado. She was also able to **reunite** with her daughter.

1. Was Clara successful in Colorado? Explain. _____

2. What did Clara do with the money she earned? _____

3. What does **reunite** mean? _____

4. What else would you like to know about Clara's life? _____

Day 4

Clara Brown and the Wagon Train

Clara Brown was born a slave. She got her freedom papers in 1857. However, Clara had only one year to leave the state. If she did not leave, the law said she would become a slave again.

At the time, African Americans could not buy tickets for public transportation. Passage on a wagon train cost about $500. Clara wanted to go west to search for her daughter Eliza. A wagon master offered her a job as a cook on his wagon train. Clara took the job.

Clara began cooking each morning at 4:00 am. Travel began by 7:00 am. The wagon train stopped for a break at noon and started traveling again at 2:00 pm. Wagons rolled until 5:00 pm. Oxen pulled the wagons. Oxen were cheaper than horses or mules. Oxen cost about $50 apiece, half of the price of a mule. Oxen pulled a loaded wagon at about two miles per hour (about 3 kph) on flat land. A wagon train traveled about 15 miles (about 24 km) a day. A train had 30 to 200 wagons. Each wagon carried up to 2,500 pounds (1,193 kg). It took Clara's wagon train about eight weeks to get to Colorado. The trip was about 680 miles (about 1,094 km). Clara walked the whole way.

1. Write a word from the passage that has a silent consonant in the middle. _____

2. What is the plural of **ox**? _____

3. What is the main idea of the first paragraph?
   A. Clara was free when she got her freedom papers.
   B. Clara got her freedom papers in 1857, but she had to leave the state or risk becoming a slave again.
   C. Clara lost her freedom papers.

4. How many minutes (or hours) do you usually walk a day? Compare that with how many hours a day Clara walked on the journey to Colorado. _____
   _____

5. Why did Clara get a job on her way out west? Compare your answer here with your answer to the same question earlier this week. _____
   _____
   _____

5.RI.1, 5.RI.2, 5.RI.3, 5.RI.4, 5.RI.5, 5.RI.6, 5.RI.7, 5.RI.8, 5.RI.9, 5.RI.10, 5.RF.3, 5.RF.4, 5.L.3, 5.L.6

Prewrite/Brainstorm

A biography is the story of a person's life. Think of someone you know and would like to write a biography about. It could be someone in your family, a friend, or a neighbor. On a separate sheet of paper, write the answers to the questions below.

1. Where and when was this person born?
2. What were the family and home of this person like?
3. Where did this person go to school?
4. What jobs has this person had?
5. What special interests, hobbies, sports, or crafts does this person enjoy?
6. What interesting things have happened to this person?

Day 1

Draft

Continue working on the biography. Look at the answers you wrote for the six questions. Draft a paragraph about that person using the information. Include a topic sentence and a conclusion. Use another sheet of paper or the computer if you want.

_____

_____

_____

_____

Day 2

Revise

Read what you wrote yesterday. Can you be more specific? Do you have information that does not support your topic sentence? Do you need to change your sentence order? Rewrite your ideas in a new paragraph.

_____

_____

_____

_____

Day 3

Proofread

Read your biography again. Do you see any capitalization errors? Are all of the words spelled correctly? Did you use the correct punctuation and grammar? Use proofreading marks to correct the sentences.

❏ Capitalization mistakes
❏ Grammar mistakes
❏ Punctuation mistakes
❏ Spelling mistakes

Day 4

Publish

Write your final copy on a computer or on the lines below.
MAKE SURE it turns out
- NEAT—Make sure there are no wrinkles, creases, or holes.
- CLEAN—Erase any smudges or dirty spots.
- EASY TO READ—Use your best handwriting and good spacing between words.

_____

_____

_____

_____

_____

_____

_____

_____

_____

_____

_____

_____

_____

_____

_____

_____

_____

_____

_____

_____

_____

_____

James Beckwourth and Fur Trading

Lewis and Clark's exploration led to fur trading in the West. Several companies competed with each other. They sold pelts around the world. They had to hire men to get furs for them. The trappers, who trapped deer, beaver, and muskrat, became known as mountain men. People of different races worked together in the fur trade.

1. What does the title tell you about the subject of this passage? _____

2. What job do you think James Beckwourth had? _____

3. Was the fur trade an equal opportunity employer? _____

4. What clues from the paragraph helped you answer question 3? _____

Day 1

One of those men was an African American named James Beckwourth. His mother was a slave. He was born in Virginia but grew up in Missouri. His father taught him to ride horses, work the land, cook, fish, and track game. He apprenticed to a blacksmith for five years. In 1818, when he was 20 years old, he began exploring the West.

1. How old was James when he became apprenticed to the blacksmith? _____

2. Name three skills James's father taught him. _____

3. Why do you think James's father taught him those things? _____

4. Which parts of the country (not the name of the state) did James live in over the course of his life? _____

Day 2

James lived with Native American tribes, and from them, he learned how to trap beaver and otter. In 1823, he worked as a scout for a fur company. In 1824, he married a Crow woman named Pine Leaf.

1. When the author says James married a Crow woman, what does that mean?
   A. Her last name was Crow.
   B. She was a member of the Native American Crow tribe.

2. What were the effects of James living with Native American tribes? _____

3. Does this paragraph tell what happens to beavers after they are trapped? _____

4. What does a scout do? _____

Day 3

James became a famous mountain man. He found a pass through the Sierra Nevada Mountains, now known as Beckwourth Pass. It was an important route for wagon trains going to California.

1. In what mountain range would you find Beckwourth Pass? _____

2. What jobs did James hold in his lifetime? _____

3. Do you consider James a hero? Why or why not? _____

4. Would you like to have had James's life? Why or why not? _____

_____

Day 4

Cowboys

In 1865, at the end of the Civil War, there were only five western states: Texas, Nevada, Oregon, Kansas, and Oklahoma. There were few towns in those states. Native Americans lived in western lands, but most of the land was still unsettled.

Slaves needed jobs after the war. At first, they went to Texas to work on cattle ranches. They called the road to Texas the Freedom Road.

From the 1870s to the 1890s, one out of every five cowboys was African American. Some saved enough money to buy their own small ranches and cattle.

Nat Love was born into a slave family in Tennessee. In 1869, he traveled to Dodge City, Kansas, hoping to become a cowboy. He drove cattle from Texas to Dodge City every spring and summer. Nat was skilled in roping, riding, and taming wild horses. During a rodeo in 1876 in South Dakota, he won every event.

George McJunkin was born a slave in Texas. He learned how to rope and ride horses from Spanish cowboys on his owner's ranch. After the Civil War, he went to New Mexico. There, he worked on ranches as a trail driver. He was skilled in breaking, or taming, wild horses. He became a wagon boss for two ranches. He was responsible for 200 horses, 1,000 cattle, and 100 Caucasian cowboys. He had always been interested in archeology. He liked to hunt for fossils. One day, he discovered the fossils of an ancient bison containing a spear point. The fossils were found to be at least 10,000 years old. His discovery proved that people lived in North America far longer than anyone had believed.

1. What do you picture when you see the title "Cowboys"? _____

   _____

2. Why did the ex-slaves call the road to Texas the Freedom Road? _____

   _____

3. Was Nat Love good at being a cowboy? What clues from the paragraph helped you answer that question? _____

   _____

4. What clues from the paragraph tell you that George McJunkin had a curious mind? _____

   _____

5. What different groups of people were cowboys? _____

   _____

Circle the choice that shows the correct capitalization.
1.   A. tuesday, january 22   B. tuesday, January 22
     C. Tuesday, January 22

Circle the correct word.
2.   (He, Him) and Brooke are (hour, our) cousins.

Mark the sentence to add the missing punctuation.
3.   Kate and Luis entered the capsule

Circle the correct word for the sentence.
4.   My dad (lies, lays) in the hammock for hours.

Day 1

Circle the choice that shows the correct capitalization.
1.   A. Our teacher is mr. Conti.   B. Our Teacher is Mr. Conti.
     C. Our teacher is Mr. Conti.

Circle the correct word.
2.   (Affects/Effects) of the earthquake are everywhere (accept, except) the shelter.

Add the missing punctuation to the sentence.
3.   What is their mission

Circle the correct word for the sentence.
4.   Michael has (lain, laid) his scissors on the desk.

Day 2

Circle the choice that shows the correct capitalization.
1.   A. *The house on the hill*   B. *The House on the Hill*
     C. *The House On the Hill*

Circle the correct word.
2.   Every one of (us, we) boys passed (their, his) test.

Mark the sentence to add the missing punctuation.
3.   Look out It's an asteroid

Circle the correct word for the sentence.
4.   The papers have (laid, lain) on the desk for weeks.

Day 3

Circle the choice that shows the correct capitalization.
1.   A. Police Chief Harry Martinez   B. Police Chief Harry martinez
     C. Police chief Harry Martinez

Circle the correct word.
2.   Donna and (I, me) helped Wendy with (she, her) homework.

Mark the sentence to add the missing punctuation.
3.   Zach calls back to the ship

Circle the correct word for the sentence.
4.   (Lay, Lie) down, Spot!

Day 4

Circle the choices that show the correct capitalization.

1. A. Fire marshall Penny Young

    B. Fire Marshall Penny Young

    C. fire marshall Penny Young

2. A. My Dog is from Pluto.

    B. My dog Is from pluto.

    C. My dog is from Pluto.

3. A. Is Mr. Brown your Teacher?

    B. Is mr. Brown your teacher?

    C. Is Mr. Brown your teacher?

Circle the correct word.

4. Richard and (she, her) did well in every subject (accept, except) history.

5. Uncle Bill thanked (us, we) children for (hour, our) concern.

Mark the sentences to add the missing punctuation.

6. They are on their way into deep space

7. Before the launch, they checked their seat belts

8. How long will it take them to get to the moon

Circle the correct word for the sentence.

9. The lion (lies, lays) quietly, waiting for its prey.

10. You can (lie, lay) your coat on the chair.

5.L.1, 5.L.2

Legend of the Cherokee Rose

In 1838, the United States Government made the Cherokee move from their homes in Georgia and other states to what was then called the Indian Territory. That land is now the state of Oklahoma.

1. What clues does the title give us about the subject of this passage? _____

2. Does the first paragraph tell us anything about who the Cherokee were? Explain.
_____

3. Does the first paragraph tell us anything about the rose in the title? _____

4. How long ago did the events in this passage take place? _____

The Cherokee had to walk for hundreds of miles, and they often did not have enough food or water. Many hundreds of them died. The mothers felt so sad that some of them could not take care of their children.

1. How did the Cherokee get to Indian Territory? _____

2. Does the author include any opinions in this paragraph? _____

3. Who is feeling sad in this paragraph? _____

4. This trip is called the Trail of Tears. What clues tell you why? _____
_____

According to the legend, the chiefs asked the Great One for a sign that would make the mothers feel better and make them strong enough to take care of their children.

1. Who in the tribe created a solution to the problem? _____

2. What solution did the tribe create for the mothers? _____

3. Who do you think the Great One was? _____

4. If you were the Great One, what kind of sign would you send to make the mothers feel better and be stronger? _____
_____

The Great One promised that where a mother's tear fell, a flower would grow. It is called the Cherokee rose. It is white, which stands for the mothers' tears. The flower's center is gold, a symbol of the gold that was taken from the tribe's land. The seven leaves on the stem stand for the seven groups who walked along the Trail of Tears.

1. What is the Cherokee rose? _____

2. How did the legend of Cherokee rose come about? _____

3. What are the different parts of the rose, and what are they symbols of? _____
_____

4. How does this story make you feel? _____

The Trail of Tears

The ancient Cherokee were hunters and farmers. They lived in the area that we know as the Appalachian Mountains of Georgia. But in 1829, white settlers found gold on this land. They went to the United States Government and asked that the Cherokee be forced to leave the land, hoping they would then get the rights to it.

A new law called the Indian Removal Act of 1830 was passed. The law stated that all Native Americans east of the Mississippi would be moved. They would have to move to territory in the West—an area that is now Oklahoma.

Some agreed to go, but most would not leave their land. Starting in the spring of 1838, the army gathered the Cherokee together. The people were held in forts like prisoners. Within one month, the first group of Cherokee was forced to leave Georgia. They marched over 1,000 miles to the new land. Some people had horses and wagons. Most people walked. The trip lasted many months. Thousands died either during the march or once they got to the land. There was no shelter or food at the territory. The last group of Cherokee arrived on the Indian Territory in March of 1839. In all, almost 17,000 Cherokee were forced to move to the new land.

1. Why were the Cherokee forced to leave? _____

_____

2. Did the Cherokee go willingly? _____

_____

3. What was the Trail of Tears? _____

_____

4. Could something like this happen today? Explain. _____

_____

_____

_____

_____

Prewrite/Brainstorm

When you write a letter, you have a purpose: You want to share or receive information or ideas. Think of a famous person whom you admire. What would you like to tell that person? Write a list of several things you would like to tell the person in a friendly letter.

_____

_____

_____

Day 1

Draft

Write a short letter to the famous person. Use the ideas you listed to create a friendly message. Be sure to include the date, a greeting, and a closing with your signature.

_____

_____

_____

_____

_____

Day 2

Revise

Read your draft letter. Do you begin with an introduction? Do you compliment the person? Does the letter conclude with a pleasant closing? Rewrite the letter.

_____

_____

_____

_____

_____

Day 3

Proofread

Read your letter again. Do you see any capitalization errors? Are all of the words spelled correctly? Did you use the correct punctuation and grammar? Use proofreading marks to correct the sentences.

- ❒ Capitalization mistakes
- ❒ Grammar mistakes
- ❒ Punctuation mistakes
- ❒ Spelling mistakes

Day 4

Publish

Write your final copy on a computer or on the lines below.
MAKE SURE it turns out

- NEAT—Make sure there are no wrinkles, creases, or holes.
- CLEAN—Erase any smudges or dirty spots.
- EASY TO READ—Use your best handwriting and good spacing between words.

_____

_____

_____

_____

_____

_____

_____

_____

_____

_____

_____

_____

_____

_____

_____

_____

_____

_____

_____

_____

The Incredible George Washington Carver

George Washington Carver was born in 1861. His parents were slaves. They lived on a plantation in Missouri.

1. What does the title tell you about the subject of this passage? _____
   _____

2. What opinion word is in the title? _____

3. Was George born into a privileged situation? _____

4. Who do you think he was named after? _____

Day 1

George Washington Carver was often sick as a child. He couldn't help around the plantation. He liked to spend time in the woods. There, he found flowers and plants. He made a collection of them. George taught himself to read. He was very independent. When he was 10 years old, he left the plantation to live on his own.

1. What was the effect of George's childhood illnesses? _____

2. What did George do instead of work on the plantation? _____

3. What is a surprising fact at the end of the paragraph? _____

4. Can you imagine leaving home and living on your own at 10 years old? Explain.
   _____

Day 2

George wanted to go to a college. The college refused to admit him because he was African American. But, George refused to give up. Finally, he went to college. He was an excellent student. He took botany and chemistry classes.

1. Does George give up easily? _____

2. What clues helped you answer question 1? _____

3. What kind of classes are botany and chemistry: **literature** or **science**? _____

4. What clues tell you whether George was a hard worker? _____
   _____

Day 3

George Washington Carver became a scientist. He discovered more than 300 uses for the peanut plant. Among his discoveries were shampoo, car grease, soap, rubber, wood filler, paint, and shoe polish. His research helped farmers.

1. What was the effect of George's research? _____

2. What character traits did George have? _____

3. What was the effect of George's plant collecting when he was a boy? _____

4. Do you agree with the author's title—is George Washington Carver incredible? Why or why not? _____

Day 4

Good News, Bad News

Most people welcome a new invention that makes life easier, but when the cotton gin arrived in 1793, it was the slaves' worst nightmare.

At that time, Southerners weren't making as much money as they wanted from their crops, especially cotton. One kind of cotton was simple to de-seed, but it thrived only near water. Another type was hard to de-seed, but it grew anywhere inland.

Eli Whitney, a Yale graduate who moved to Georgia, sized up the cotton situation. Within a short time, this brilliant young man invented the cotton gin. The gin detached the seeds from the soft, cottony fibers. The sturdy, inland cotton could quickly be de-seeded. The machine was unbelievably simple and used wires, a drum, and a brush.

Growing cotton could now make a lot of money for the plantation owners. They stopped grumbling and began exporting cotton and importing slaves. Who else could work the fields? Who else could pick the large amounts of cotton that were fed into the supermachine?

Between 1790 and 1808, 80,000 Africans were shipped to the South. The cotton gin helped the South produce 75 percent of the cotton the world used. The Southerners wanted an important crop to export, and now they had one. In 1860, the South produced around 5 million bales of cotton. Sadly, about one-third of the people in the South were slaves that same year.

All Eli Whitney wanted was to make life easier. Instead, life for thousands became much harder.

1. What was the **good** news? _____

2. What was the **bad** news? _____

3. What is the author's opinion of Eli Whitney? _____
   _____

4. What is the author's opinion of the invention of the cotton gin? _____
   _____

5.RI.1, 5.RI.2, 5.RI.3, 5.RI.4, 5.RI.5, 5.RI.6, 5.RI.7, 5.RI.8, 5.RI.9, 5.RI.10, 5.RF.3, 5.RF.4, 5.L.3, 5.L.4, 5.L.5, 5.L.6   CD-104600 • © Carson-Dellosa

Underline with three short lines the first letter of words that need to be capitalized.
1.   did the movie *around the world in 80 days* win an academy award in 1956?

Draw a line under the complete predicate. Circle the predicate verb.
2.   Jayla and I cheered for our favorite team.

Add quotation marks, capitalization, underlines, and punctuation where necessary in the sentence.
3.   The Olympic Games were held in Stockholm Sweden in 1912 replied valerie

Circle the correct words in the sentence.
4.   My library book was (dew/due) last (week/weak).

Underline with three short lines the first letter of words that need to be capitalized.
1.   robert burns, the poet, wrote "auld lang syne."

Draw a line under the complete predicate. Circle the predicate verb.
2.   Chris dropped one more quarter into the machine.

Add quotation marks, capitalization, underlines, and punctuation where necessary in the sentence.
3.   Monica yelled Wow did you see that car

Circle the correct words in the sentence.
4.   Did those (ate/eight) (flowers/flours) come from your yard?

Underline with three short lines the first letter of words that need to be capitalized.
1.   does grandpa get the *chicago sun-times* or the *chicago tribune*?

Draw a line under the complete predicate. Circle the predicate verb.
2.   The clerk examined the jacket carefully.

Add quotation marks, capitalization, underlines, and punctuation where necessary in the sentence.
3.   Look out screamed Andrew

Circle the correct words in the sentence.
4.   Fiona (scent/sent) her (aunt/ant) a birthday card.

Underline with three short lines the first letter of words that need to be capitalized.
1.   we're going to an italian restaurant on friday night after we read *strega nona*.

Draw a line under the complete predicate. Circle the predicate verb.
2.   Maddie's dog, Bandit, is a frisky animal.

Add quotation marks, capitalization, underlines, and punctuation where necessary in the sentence.
3.   Bobbi our class president took charge of today's meeting

Circle the correct words in the sentence.
4.   (Too/To/Two) dollars is a (fare/fair) price.

Day 1

Day 2

Day 3

Day 4

Using proofreading marks, mark the first letter of words that need to be capitalized and add punctuation to the sentences.

1.   i received the book *the life cycle book of cats* from grandmother

2.   will judge j.t. ormand preside today

3.   dad, *the los angeles times* was not delivered this morning said dave

4.   dions deli carries turkish candy remarked penny

Draw a line under the complete predicate in the sentences. Circle the predicate verb.

5.   My teacher asked for volunteers.

6.   The birds ate all of the seeds.

7.   Rick and I are in the same race.

Circle the correct words in the sentences.

8.   Dad (sent/scent) Mom (flowers/flours) for her birthday.

9.   We have (too/two) more (weeks/weaks) until this is (due/dew).

10.   Can you imagine having (eight/ate) uncles and (ants/aunts)?

The Underground Railroad

The Underground Railroad wasn't a railroad at all. It was a group of people who helped slaves escape to freedom. Those in charge of the escape effort were often called **conductors**. The people escaping were known as **passengers**. And the places where the escaping slaves stopped for help were often called **stations**.

1. What does the title tell you the subject of the passage might be? _____

2. Does the opening sentence **support** or **contradict** your guess? _____

3. What kind of railroad is the passage about? _____

4. What does the opening paragraph tell us about who is involved? _____

Like a train ride, the Underground Railroad moved people along. Those who escaped often followed routes that had been laid out by others before them. However, unlike a train ride, some routes went underground through dirt tunnels without any sort of tracks.

1. What comparison does this paragraph make? _____

2. How is the subject like the thing it's compared with? _____

3. How is the subject unlike the thing it's compared with? _____

4. How does this paragraph make you feel? _____

Escaping slaves had to be certain that they could find their way. They needed food and water to make the journey. Conductors helped guide them and provide supplies. One of the most famous Underground Railroad conductors was Harriet Tubman. She had escaped slavery herself. Another famous conductor was Levi Coffin.

1. What part of the subject does this paragraph focus on? _____

2. Name two famous conductors. _____

3. What was their job? _____

4. What details did you discover about one of the conductors? _____

_____

Experts disagree about how well the Underground Railroad was organized. Still, it is believed that the system helped thousands of slaves reach freedom between 1830 and 1865.

1. What problem did the Underground Railroad try to solve? _____

2. What new details did you learn? _____

3. How many years did the Underground Railroad operate? _____

4. Imagine traveling the Underground Railroad. Do you imagine yourself as a slave or a conductor? _____

Day 1

Day 2

Day 3

Day 4

Sewing to Slavery, Sewing to Freedom

Many African women were skillful seamstresses. Many of them knew how to sew before they were brought to America as slaves. Skillful seamstresses sold for a high price on the slavery block. Sometimes, they sold for as much as $1,000.

Some slaves made quilts for their owners. They used the scraps from those quilts to make quilts to keep their own families warm. Those quilts often told the stories of their families. The quilts were called story quilts.

One slave named Elizabeth Keckley used her sewing skill to earn her freedom. In 1855, she earned $1,200, enough to buy her freedom. As a free woman, she sewed for President Lincoln's wife. She earned enough money to support 17 people.

1. What was the effect of a slave's ability to sew? _____

_____

2. How could sewing help free a slave like Elizabeth Keckley? _____

_____

3. What was a story quilt? _____

_____

4. Why was a story quilt important to a slave family? _____

_____

Name_____

Prewrite/Brainstorm

A paragraph that tells how things are the same or different is called a compare-and-contrast paragraph. Using the Venn diagram, write your idea about how living in the city is different from or the same as living in the country.

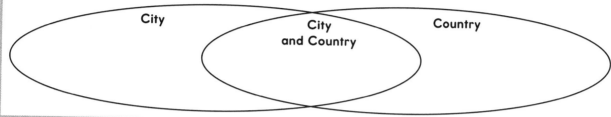

Draft

Use the information you wrote in the Venn diagram to write a compare-and-contrast paragraph about living in the city or country. Remember to include a topic sentence and a conclusion statement.

_____

_____

_____

_____

Revise

Look at your draft. Did you begin with a topic sentence? Did you use specific words to describe similarities and differences? Did you use a conclusion sentence? Rewrite your paragraph with more specific words.

_____

_____

_____

_____

Proofread

Read your paragraph again. Do you see any capitalization errors? Are all of the words spelled correctly? Did you use the correct punctuation and grammar? Use proofreading marks to correct the sentences.

- ❏ Capitalization mistakes
- ❏ Grammar mistakes
- ❏ Punctuation mistakes
- ❏ Spelling mistakes

Publish

Write your final copy on a computer or on the lines below.
MAKE SURE it turns out
- NEAT—Make sure there are no wrinkles, creases, or holes.
- CLEAN—Erase any smudges or dirty spots.
- EASY TO READ—Use your best handwriting and good spacing between words.

_____

_____

_____

_____

_____

_____

_____

_____

_____

_____

_____

_____

_____

_____

_____

_____

_____

_____

5.W.2, 5.W.4, 5.W.5, 5.W.6, 5.W.10, 5.L.1, 5.L.2

Aboriginal Art

The Aboriginal people in Australia are hunters and gatherers. They are also skilled artists. They have been painting and carving rocks for thousands of years. The paintings are found mostly in caves throughout central Australia. The oldest paintings that have been discovered are about 30,000 years old.

1. What does the title tell us about the subject of this passge? _____

2. Where do Aborigines live? _____

3. What details does the first paragraph tell you about them? _____

4. Aborigines are the original dwellers of Australia. Who do they compare with in the United States? _____

Day 1

Aborigine artists still use natural paints made from the earth, tree bark, and plants. Red comes from ochre and hematite. Ochre and hematite are minerals. Black comes from charcoal. White comes from gypsum, a mineral found in rocks. It's used to make cement.

1. Where do Aborigine artists find their paints? _____

2. What color does not come from a mineral? _____

3. Does this paragraph give you any examples of colors from plants? _____

4. What do Aboriginal paintings have in common with cement? _____

Day 2

Aborigine musicians have unusual musical instruments. One is called the didgeridoo. It is made from a hollowed-out log. It is a wind instrument played by blowing air through it. A didgeridoo may be painted with the same elaborate designs found in the rock paintings.

1. So far, in this passage, what two things do Aborigine artists paint on?_____

2. Do you think the didgeridoo is a small or a large instrument? Why?_____
   _____

3. Did Aborigine musicians find their musical instruments in nature? _____

4. What clues helped you answer question 3? _____

Day 3

Aborigines paint themselves for special religious ceremonies. These ceremonies are a part of their traditional culture. Their religion links them to the land and nature. They express themselves artistically through music making, dancing, singing, and storytelling.

1. List the things Aborigine artists paint. _____

2. What is important to their religion? _____

3. What do Aborigines do in their religious ceremonies? _____
   _____

4. How is painting used in their religious ceremonies? _____

Day 4

Dreamtime

Many cultures have stories telling how the world was created. The Aborigines believe that spirits created the world in a time known as Dreamtime. The Aborigines have lived in Australia for thousands of years. Some scientists believe they have been in Australia for about 30,000 years. The name Aborigine means "the very first." The Aborigines were the very first people in Australia. Today, the elders pass on the Dreamtime stories to younger generations.

Stories from Dreamtime explain the beginning of the world. Aborigines believe that spirits created the land, animals, plants, and people. The spirits then continued to live in nature. The spirits also live within the Aboriginal beliefs and sacred rituals. Dreamtime stories tell more than the origin of the world, they explain the rules for living. They explain the rules for behavior and society.

Dreamtime paintings show stories from Dreamtime. The paintings are usually symmetrical. They are made of arcs, circles, and ovals. Some lines are straight. Other lines are curved. The men paint Dreamtime symbols and patterns on their bodies for special ceremonies.

1. What is Dreamtime? _____

    _____

2. Is Dreamtime still a part of Aboriginal culture today? Explain. _____

    _____

    _____

3. Describe Dreamtime paintings. _____

    _____

    _____

4. Compare this passage to another creation story you have heard. _____

    _____

    _____

    _____

    _____

5.RI.1, 5.RI.2, 5.RI.3, 5.RI.4, 5.RI.5, 5.RI.6, 5.RI.7, 5.RI.8, 5.RI.9, 5.RI.10, 5.RF.4, 5.L.3, 5.L.4

Prewrite/Brainstorm

News stories contain specific facts that explain the five W's. Write a news story about Dreamtime using the information from Week 33.

Who? _____

What? _____

When? _____

Where? _____

Why? _____

Draft

Write a headline from the information you collected above. Then, write an article telling about the headline. Begin with a good lead that draws the reader in.

_____

_____

_____

_____

Revise

Read your news story. Did you include all five W's? Is the most important fact in the beginning of your story? Is the least important fact at the end? Did you use transition words between sentences? Rewrite the story.

_____

_____

_____

_____

Proofread

Read your news story again. Do you see any capitalization errors? Are all of the words spelled correctly? Did you use the correct punctuation and grammar? Use proofreading marks to correct the sentences.

❏ Capitalization mistakes
❏ Grammar mistakes
❏ Punctuation mistakes
❏ Spelling mistakes

Publish

Write your final copy on a computer or on the lines below.
MAKE SURE it turns out

- NEAT—Make sure there are no wrinkles, creases, or holes.
- CLEAN—Erase any smudges or dirty spots.
- EASY TO READ—Use your best handwriting and good spacing between words.

_____

_____

_____

_____

_____

_____

_____

_____

_____

_____

_____

_____

_____

_____

_____

_____

_____

_____

_____

_____

_____

_____

Each year, the citizens of the United States **celebrate** two holidays to remember men and women who fought in wars to preserve our freedom. Memorial Day is celebrated on the last Monday in May, and Veterans Day is celebrated on November 11.

1. What is the silent consonant pair in this paragraph? _____

2. Circle the synonym for **celebrated** as it is used here: **partied** or **observed**.

3. Which sentence is the topic sentence? _____

4. Which holiday has a date that is relative (the date we observe depends on another factor)? _____

Day 1

Memorial Day began after the American Civil War, when people began decorating the graves of soldiers who had died in the war. Although many claim to have started the tradition, Congress declared Waterloo, New York, the birthplace of Memorial Day when the whole community held a celebration on May 5, 1866.

1. Find a compound word in this paragraph. _____

2. What is a grave? _____

3. What is the date of the first **Memorial Day**? _____

4. How do you celebrate Memorial Day? _____
_____

Day 2

In 1868, the Grand Army of the Republic organized a ceremony at the National Cemetery in Arlington, Virginia. They called it Decoration Day because they decorated the graves of soldiers. The name was changed to Memorial Day in remembrance of men and women who gave their lives for the **freedom** of the United States.

1. Find an example of alliteration in this paragraph. _____

2. What word is the opposite of **freedom**? _____

3. Restate the last sentence in your own words. _____

4. Do you think we should combine the two holidays into one? Why or why not? _____
_____

Day 3

On November 11, 1918, a treaty was signed between Germany and the Allied forces of the United States, France, Great Britain, Russia, and Italy, putting an end to World War I. It was first called Armistice Day, but it is now called Veterans Day.

1. How do you pronounce the **ss** in **Russia**? _____

2. What does **armistice** mean?
   B. Declaration of the winner of the battle
   A. Beginning of war
   C. Parties agree to end war

3. Which two words would you emphasize in the last sentence? _____

4. Name the Allied forces who signed the treaty. _____
_____

Day 4

The Statue of Liberty

The Statue of Liberty is a symbol of freedom and welcome to the world. Frédéric Bartholdi of France sculpted the statue. It was a gift from France to the United States. The statue symbolized friendship between the two countries. It was also intended to honor the birthday of the United States' independence. President Grover Cleveland dedicated the statue in 1886. It became a national monument in 1924. The statue is located on Liberty Island in New York Harbor.

The original name for the statue was Liberty Enlightening the World. The statue's torch is a welcome symbol to immigrants. The crown has seven rays. They symbolize the seven oceans and the seven continents. Liberty has a tablet in her left hand. It shows the date July 4, 1776. The broken chain at her feet symbolizes freedom. Her Greek robe symbolizes Greece as the birthplace of democracy.

Liberty stands on a pedestal. Americans had to raise money to pay for the pedestal. Joseph Pulitzer was editor of *The World*, a New York newspaper. He thought the statue was a great idea. His newspaper ran articles about raising money for the statue. He published the names of people who gave money. He even listed the names of children who sent pennies. Americans raised $250,000. That was enough money to pay for the pedestal.

1. What are the prefix, root, and suffixes in **Enlightening**? _____

   _____

2. What is a symbol?

   A. An image that stands for an idea

   B. A part of a drum kit

   C. A statue

3. What is the main idea of paragraph 2? _____

   _____

4. What is the symbol for the oceans and continents? _____

5. Would you have sent in pennies to pay for the pedestal? Why or why not? _____

   _____

5.RI.1, 5.RI.2, 5.RI.4, 5.RI.10, 5.RF.3, 5.RF.4, 5.L.4 CD-104600 • © Carson-Dellosa

Prewrite/Brainstorm

To write a report you must first decide on a topic. Write your topic in the middle circle of the cluster map. Brainstorm subtopics and write them in the outer circles. Then, research information on the Internet about your topic and subtopics. Take notes about each subtopic.

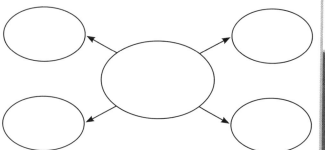

Day 1

Draft

Write an introduction paragraph about your topic below. Your paragraph should include general information about the topic and tell the reader about the subtopics that will follow. You will write about your subtopics in the weeks to come.

_____

_____

_____

_____

Day 2

Revise

Read your introduction paragraph. Do you need to put your sentences in a different order? Ask someone else to read your paragraph and make suggestions on how to improve it. Revise your paragraph with the changes you made.

_____

_____

_____

_____

Day 3

Proofread

Read your paragraph again. Do you see any capitalization errors? Are all of the words spelled correctly? Did you use the correct punctuation and grammar? Use proofreading marks to correct the sentences.

❑ Capitalization mistakes
❑ Grammar mistakes
❑ Punctuation mistakes
❑ Spelling mistakes

Day 4

Publish

Write your final copy on a computer or on the lines below.

MAKE SURE it turns out

- NEAT—Make sure there are no wrinkles, creases, or holes.
- CLEAN—Erase any smudges or dirty spots.
- EASY TO READ—Use your best handwriting and good spacing between words.

_____

_____

_____

_____

_____

_____

_____

_____

_____

_____

_____

_____

_____

_____

_____

_____

_____

_____

_____

_____

A tarantula is a big, hairy spider. You might see one in a pet shop that carries unusual pets. In the United States, tarantulas live in the West where it is hot and dry. During the day, tarantulas sleep in holes and other dark places.

1. What word above has a **t** that is pronounced like **ch**? _____

2. Give antonyms for **big, hairy**. _____

3. If you visit a pet shop that carries unusual pets, you might see
   A. a cat.   B. a canary.   C. a tarantula.

4. What might happen if you stuck your hand in a dark hole in Arizona? _____
   _____

Tarantulas catch their food mostly by jumping on it and biting it. Smaller tarantulas eat insects. Larger ones eat mice and lizards. A tarantula's poison can kill the animals it hunts, but its poison cannot kill a human.

1. Circle the word that has an ending sound like the second **t** in **tarantula**.

2. What is another word for "the animals it hunts"?
   A. Prey   B. Toast   C. Pray

3. What information in this paragraph might make you feel better about meeting a tarantula? _____

4. What kills the animals when a tarantula hunts? _____

If you are bitten, you soon know that a tarantula bite hurts only about as much as a bee sting. Its bite helps the spider protect itself. The shy tarantula bites humans only if it feels threatened and cannot get away.

1. Is the **i** in **bite** pronounced the same as the **i** in **bitten**? _____

2. What is another word that means the same as **shy**? _____

3. What might happen to someone who has been bitten by a tarantula? _____
   _____

4. Poking or touching a tarantula might make it
   A. run away.   B. bite you.   C. run until it catches you.

A tarantula has another way to protect itself. It can rub its hind legs together, which causes its stiff leg hairs to fly up in the air. Each tiny hair can cause a hurtful skin or eye wound.

1. Circle all of the words that have a short **i** sound.

2. Which meaning of **wound** is correct here: **wrapped around** or **injury**? _____

3. What details does the writer use to describe tarantula hairs? _____

4. If you looked closely at a tarantula rubbing its hind legs together, what might happen? _____

Day 1

Day 2

Day 3

Day 4

Venus Flytrap

Kayla got a **Venus flytrap** for her birthday. She put it with her other plants on her windowsill. She watered all of her plants each day.

After a week, all of her plants looked fine except for the Venus flytrap. She decided that she needed more information on this plant, so she went to the library and found a book about the Venus flytrap.

She was surprised to find out that this plant was **carnivorous**, or meat eating. No wonder it was not doing well! The book said that the Venus flytrap is a popular house plant. Each set of leaves stays open until an insect or piece of meat lands on the inside of the leaves. The two leaves close quickly, trapping the bait inside. After a leaf digests the meat, it dies. A new leaf grows to take the place of the dead leaf.

Now, Kayla knew how to take care of her Venus flytrap.

1. What clues can you get from the compound word in the name of the **Venus flytrap** about what it might eat? _____

_____

2. What does the word **carnivorous** mean? _____

_____

_____

3. Why did Kayla need to go to the library? _____

_____

_____

4. Compare this passage to a report on Venus flytraps. _____

_____

_____

Prewrite/Brainstorm

In Week 36, you wrote an introduction paragraph of a report. To continue writing your report, you must decide what you want to write in your supporting paragraphs. Use your notes from Week 36 to brainstorm what you will write in your next two paragraphs.

_____

_____

_____

Day 1

Draft

Draft the next two paragraphs. Each paragraph should be about one idea that supports your topic. Use the ideas you created when you brainstormed to help you.

_____

_____

_____

_____

Day 2

Revise

Read your supporting paragraphs. Do you need to put your sentences in a different order? Share your writing with someone. Ask for ways your writing could be improved.

_____

_____

_____

_____

Day 3

Proofread

Read your paragraphs again. Do you see any capitalization errors? Are all of the words spelled correctly? Did you use the correct punctuation and grammar? Use proofreading marks to correct the sentences.

❏ Capitalization mistakes
❏ Grammar mistakes
❏ Punctuation mistakes
❏ Spelling mistakes

Day 4

Publish

Add these two paragraphs to the introduction paragraph you wrote on a computer or on the lines below.

MAKE SURE it turns out

- NEAT—Make sure there are no wrinkles, creases, or holes.
- CLEAN—Erase any smudges or dirty spots.
- EASY TO READ—Use your best handwriting and good spacing between words.

_____

_____

_____

_____

_____

_____

_____

_____

_____

_____

_____

_____

_____

_____

_____

_____

_____

_____

_____

They call me a three-toed **sloth**, but everyone definitely knows
When you count them all up, I have 12 gorgeous toes.

1. Is **sloth** pronounced more like **both** or **broth**? _____

2. What word could you use instead of **count**: **add** or **multiply**? _____

3. From whose point of view is this piece written? _____

4. What genre of writing is this? _____

I require splendid, tropical rain forests in order to **survive**,
For if it weren't for them, I most certainly wouldn't be alive.

1. What does **survive** mean? _____

2. What fact do you learn about a three-toed sloth in this stanza? _____

3. Who does the pronoun **I** refer to? _____ What about the pronoun **them**?

   _____

4. Would a three-toed sloth be found in the deserts of the United States? Explain.

   _____

I'm a downright lazy mammal who's never in a hurry.
My natural coat is brownish green and really very furry.

1. Write the compound word in this stanza. _____

2. What two facts do you learn about a three-toed sloth in this stanza? _____

   _____

3. If you were to see a sloth in its natural environment, what would you expect to see?

   _____

4. Write a simile describing the speed of a sloth. _____

I am a lazy animal who sleeps all through the day.
I **feast** only on green plants, and I like it just that way.

1. Is the sloth a carnivore or an herbivore? _____

2. What two facts do you learn about a three-toed sloth in this stanza? _____

   _____

3. What is a synonym for **feast** as it is used in this poem? _____

4. What is the rhyme scheme of this poem?

   A. aa bb cc dd   B. ab ab cd cd   C. Free verse

Love Unreturned

You are my love, my love you are.
I worship you from afar;
I, through the branches, spy you.

You are a climbing ace.
But, I do not like your fuzzy face.
Away from me, please take you!

I love your ears, so soft and tall.
I love your nose, so pink and small.
I must make you my own bride!

I will not climb, I cannot eat
the acorns that you call a treat.
Now, shimmy up that tree and hide!

Oh grant me peace, my love.
Climb to my home so far above
the place you call your warren.

I like my home in the tree's hollow
where fox and weasel may not follow—
a place below your tree house so barren.

I must stay on the lovely ground
with carrots and cabbages all around.
I long for a garden, not a tree.

Alas, I hide up in my bower,
Lonesome still, I shake and cower.
Sadness overtakes me.

1. Who is the speaker in love? _____

2. Who is the speaker who does not return the love? _____

3. What is the rhyme scheme in this poem?

    A. aba / cbc

    B. abb / cbb

    C. aab / ccb

4. If you wrote a report about these two animals, what factual information could you get from this poem? _____

    _____

    _____

Prewrite/Brainstorm

To finish the report you worked on in Week 36 and Week 38, write two additional supporting paragraphs and a concluding paragraph. Use your notes from Week 36. Brainstorm what you will write.

_____

_____

_____

_____

Day 1

Draft

Use the ideas you brainstormed to draft your final paragraphs. Your concluding paragraph should sum up your report.

_____

_____

_____

_____

Day 2

Revise

Read what you have written. Do you need to put your sentences in a different order? Ask someone to read your paragraph and make suggestions for improvement. Rewrite your ideas in a new paragraph.

_____

_____

_____

_____

Day 3

Proofread

Read your paragraphs again. Do you see any capitalization errors? Are all of the words spelled correctly? Did you use the correct punctuation and grammar? Use proofreading marks to correct the sentences.

❏ Capitalization mistakes
❏ Grammar mistakes
❏ Punctuation mistakes
❏ Spelling mistakes

Day 4

Publish

Add your final paragraphs to your report on a computer or on the lines below.
MAKE SURE it turns out
- NEAT—Make sure there are no wrinkles, creases, or holes.
- CLEAN—Erase any smudges or dirty spots.
- EASY TO READ—Use your best handwriting and good spacing between words.

_____

_____

_____

_____

_____

_____

_____

_____

_____

_____

_____

_____

_____

_____

_____

_____

_____

_____

_____

_____

Answer Key

Page 9
Day 1: 1. a lazy time; 2. a swaying swing; 3. to rock back and forth; 4. Answers will vary. **Day 2:** 1. autumn; 2. Air is crisp and leaves are falling. 3. a dog; 4. His body is shaggy and he licks Sally's hand. **Day 3:** 1. geese honk, mom calls, dog barks; 2. an older dog; 3. graying ears; 4. dinner; **Day 4:** 1. Answers will vary. 2. Answers will vary but may include: swaying slowly, snuggles, sluggish, drifts, slowly turns. 3. Answers will vary. 4. Answers will vary.

Page 10
1. names of chapters and what pages they begin on; 2. chronologically; 3. autumn; 4. at the lake; 5. Answers will vary.

Page 11
Day 1: 1. Dad, I, park; 2. It's; 3. graders'; 4. wait, who's; **Day 2:** 1. The, Benjamin's, group; 2. there, too; 3. car's; That's; 4. Which, favorite; **Day 3:** 1. Nguyen's, kindergarten; 2. your, there; 3. they're, car's; 4. because, apart; **Day 4:** 1. Did, Mr.; 2. It's; 3. I'm, year's; 4. pleased, surprised, piece

Page 12
Day 1: Buster's, He's, pond, Dad, That's, because, surprised, you're, wait, Your

Page 13
Day 1: 1. C; 2. They are a fox and a crow. 3. No. They are acting like animals. 4. perched on a limb to eat it; **Day 2:** 1. You look lovely. I bet your voice is just as beautiful. 2. a loud, irritating caw; 3. to get her to open her mouth and drop the cheese; 4. afternoon; **Day 3:** 1. because she wanted to show off her singing; 2. No, he was trying to get the cheese; 3. ate it; 4. He devoured it; **Day 4:** 1. Answers will vary. 2. C; 3. Answers will vary. 4. Answers will vary.

Page 14
1. Accept any reasonable answer. 2. plants; 3. Oak trees are large, sturdy trees; reeds are tall, flexible grass. 4. A; 5. Answers will vary, although a nonfiction article would include more factual information and would not include a story.

Page 15
Day 1: The brainstorming activity should contain various ideas or words related to the topic. **Day 2:** The first draft should contain ideas taken from the brainstorming activity and use either first- or third-person narration consistently. **Day 3:** The next draft should show improvements in clarity and consistency of the point of view. **Day 4:** The final draft should show proofreading marks where needed.

Page 16
The content of writing samples will vary. Check to be sure that students have correctly completed all of the earlier steps in the writing process and have followed instructions for publishing their work.

Page 17
Day 1: 1. the author's best friend; 2. He has never been waterskiing, but he is a good athlete; 3. easy; 4. author's use of the words "I thought"; **Day 2:** 1. The author loves waterskiing. 2. the use of the words "like an eagle in flight"; 3. Answers will vary but may include words such as *majestic* or *powerful.* 4. a large bird; **Day 3:** 1. a weight to keep a boat from moving; 2. because he sinks; 3. "sank like an anchor" and "flipping head over heels like a gymnast"; 4. Answers will vary, but look for a comparison using *like* or *as.* **Day 4:** 1. "teetered back and forth like a rag doll" and "flopped at the end of the rope like a fish"; 2. Answers will vary. 3. metaphor; 4. Answers will vary.

Page 18
1. a cat; 2. Answers will vary. 3. "tongue, like fine grains of sand on paper"; 4. "She is an electric sander" and "She is a nail file."

Page 19
Day 1: The brainstorming activity should contain various ideas or words related to the topic. **Day 2:** The first draft should contain ideas taken from the brainstorming activity written in quatrains. **Day 3:** The next draft should show improvements in organization and detail. **Day 4:** The final draft should show proofreading marks where needed.

Page 20
The content of writing samples will vary. Check to be sure that students have correctly completed all of the earlier steps in the writing process and have followed instructions for publishing their work.

Page 21
Day 1: 1. Chinese; 2. A; 3. a traditional Chinese meal; 4. no; **Day 2:** 1. dizzy; 2. aroma; 3. six; 4. two; **Day 3:** 1. wok, walk; 2. a large pan used in Chinese cooking; 3. sizzle; 4. with a knife and fork; **Day 4:** 1. shus; 2. healthful; 3. (circled) rice; 4. no

Page 22
1. chopsticks; 2. a prediction; 3. clicking, splash; 4. She comforted her and gave her a knife and fork. 5. Answers will vary.

Page 23
Day 1: The brainstorming activity should contain various ideas or words related to the topic. **Day 2:** The first draft should contain ideas taken from the brainstorming activity including a problem. **Day 3:** The next draft should show improvements in organization and detail. **Day 4:** The final draft should show proofreading marks where needed.

Page 24
The content of writing samples will vary. Check to be sure that students have correctly completed all of the earlier steps in the writing process and have followed instructions for publishing their work.

Page 25
Day 1: 1. The title "Understudy" and "but the lead actress had not arrived"; 2. Beth; 3. the problem of the missing lead actress; 4. Answers will vary. **Day 2:** 1. "put a damper on things" and "eggs in one basket"; 2. calmly told Amanda to take Beth's place; 3. yes; 4. She knows the part well. **Day 3:** 1. "on cloud nine" and "the apple of my eye"; 2. Yes. She was on cloud nine. 3. She didn't know how to respond; 4. Answers will vary. **Day 4:** 1. her dad and grandpa, but there were others; 2. "raining cats and dogs," "keep an eye on," "slower than molasses in January," and "by the skin of my teeth"; 3. Answers will vary. 4. Answers will vary.

Page 26
1. (underlined) out of the blue, fly the coop, hold a candle to her, my foot in my mouth, cat got your tongue, had me over a barrel, drop it, one-track mind, sitting duck, all ears, too big for her britches; 2A. hold a candle to; B. out of the blue; C. fly the coop; D. foot in my mouth; 3. Answers will vary. 4. Answers will vary.

Page 27
Day 1: The brainstorming activity should contain various ideas or words related to the topic. **Day 2:** The first draft should contain ideas taken from the brainstorming activity. **Day 3:** The next draft should show improvements in organization and detail. **Day 4:** The final draft should show proofreading marks where needed.

Page 28
The content of writing samples will vary. Check to be sure that students have correctly completed all of the earlier steps in the writing process and have followed instructions for publishing their work.

Page 29
Day 1: 1. root – forget; suffix – ful; 2. forgets easily; 3. loudly; with excitement; 4. A; **Day 2:** 1. (circled) gingerbread; 2. cancelled; 3. Answers will vary. 4. She mentioned the girls' gym; **Day 3:** 1. misplace; 2. mis/place; 3. loudly; 4. Her name is Tara. **Day 4:** 1. geography; 2. writing about the earth; 3. no; 4. She usually gets A's.

Page 30
1. build; 2. responsible for the crime; 3. excitement; 4. Yes. She said it was incredible and wanted Tara to read it to the class. 5. She forgot she had turned in her report early.

Page 31
Day 1: The brainstorming activity should contain various ideas or words related to the topic. **Day 2:** The first draft should contain ideas taken from the brainstorming activity. **Day 3:** The next draft should show improvements in organization and detail. **Day 4:** The final draft should show proofreading marks where needed.

CD-104600 • © Carson-Dellosa

Page 32
The content of writing samples will vary. Check to be sure that students have correctly completed all of the earlier steps in the writing process and have followed instructions for publishing their work.

Page 33
Day 1: 1. Australian animals; 2. nonfiction; 3. They give birth by laying eggs. 4. They carry their babies in pouches. **Day 2:** 1. marsupial; 2. It lives on the island of Tasmania. 3. carnivore; 4. Answers will vary. **Day 3:** 1. monotreme; 2. beaver; 3. Answers will vary. 4. Answers will vary. **Day 4:** 1. B; 2. marsupial; 3. hops on hind legs; 4. Answers will vary.

Page 34
1. Australia and the United States will be compared.; 2. Answers will vary. 3. Answers will vary.

Page 35
Day 1: The brainstorming activity should contain various ideas or words related to the topic with differences in the outer circles and likenesses in the intersecting section. **Day 2:** The first draft should contain ideas taken from the brainstorming activity. **Day 3:** The next draft should show improvements in organization and detail. **Day 4:** The final draft should show proofreading marks where needed.

Page 36
The content of writing samples will vary. Check to be sure that students have correctly completed all of the earlier steps in the writing process and have followed instructions for publishing their work.

Page 37
Day 1: 1. It's about an opera house in Sydney. 2. no; 3. yes; 4. A harbor is on the water. **Day 2:** 1. yes. Australia; 2. 14 years; 3. $7 million (Australian); 4. No. It was $95 million off the estimate. **Day 3:** 1. no; 2. Some people think it looks like seashells. 3. concrete; 4. The concrete was heavy and could drop. **Day 4:** 1. 3/5; 2. B; 3. Answers will vary. 4. Answers will vary.

Page 38
1. nonfiction; 2. by describing a storm at sea; 3. to guide ships into coastal waters; 4. Answers will vary but may include something about ships being the only transportation between the continents at the time.

Page 39
Day 1: The brainstorming activity should contain various ideas or words related to the topic completing the graphic organizer. **Day 2:** The first draft should contain ideas taken from the graphic organizer. **Day 3:** The next draft should show improvements in organization and detail. **Day 4:** The final draft should show proofreading marks where needed.

Page 40
The content of writing samples will vary. Check to be sure that students have correctly completed all of the earlier steps in the writing process and have followed instructions for publishing their work.

Page 41
Day 1: 1. (circled) vegetables, oranges, vegetables; (underlined) Green, sugar, sugar, sugar; 2. factories; 3. a place where things are made; 4. sugar and starch; **Day 2:** 1. chloroplasts, chlorophyll; 2. tool for looking at small objects; 3. the cells of a living organism; 4. no; **Day 3:** 1. (circled) Roots, root; (underlined) doors, door; 2. tiny holes in plant leaves; 3. Doors of the Factory; 4. stomata and roots; **Day 4:** 1. (circled) storerooms; 2. keep, save; 3. (underlined) Plants use storerooms to store their food. 4. carrot->root; lettuce->leaves; peas->seeds; peach tree->fruit; maple tree->trunk

Page 42
1. The brain sorts out information and lets the body know what to do. 2. by the three parts of the brain; 3. It tells the body what to do like a coach tells the players. 4. A. cerebrum; B. cerebellum; C. medulla oblongata

Page 43

Day 1: The brainstorming activity should contain various ideas or words related to the topic completing the graphic organizer. **Day 2:** The first draft should contain ideas taken from the graphic organizer. **Day 3:** The next draft should show improvements in organization and detail. **Day 4:** The final draft should show proofreading marks where needed.

Page 44

The content of writing samples will vary. Check to be sure that students have correctly completed all of the earlier steps in the writing process and have followed instructions for publishing their work.

Page 45

Day 1: 1. It will be about television. 2. Yes; it will be about the invention of the television. 3. Answers will vary. 4. The invention of the television changed the world in many important ways. **Day 2:** 1. radio; 2. about 100 years; 3. the electronic television camera; 4. about 100 years; **Day 3:** 1. the iconoscope and the kinescope; 2. the United States; 3. Answers will vary. 4. Answers will vary. **Day 4:** 1. three; 2. Light and sound waves are changed into electronic signals, electronic signals pass through the air to the TV set, the TV unscrambles the signals; 3. light and sound waves; 4. Answers will vary.

Page 46

1. Philo Farnsworth; 2. Farnsworth's childhood; 3. Farnsworth's education; 4. invention of the television; 5. Farnsworth's honors

Page 47

Day 1: The brainstorming activity should contain various ideas or words related to the topic and considering the audience. **Day 2:** The first draft should contain ideas taken from the brainstorming activity and keeping in mind the audience. **Day 3:** The next draft should show improvements in organization and detail and attracting the audience. **Day 4:** The final draft should show proofreading marks where needed.

Page 48

The content of writing samples will vary. Check to be sure that students have correctly completed all of the earlier steps in the writing process and have followed instructions for publishing their work.

Page 49

Day 1: 1. peer; 2. The author likes hair. 3. The author makes it personal. 4. information about hair; **Day 2:** 1. second; 2. shield, deter, trap, prevent; 3. sweat; 4. eyebrows and eyelashes; **Day 3:** 1. first; 2. a tube growing out of a hair root; 3. a stack of dead hair cells; 4. root, follicle, hair shaft; **Day 4:** 1. Answers will vary. 2. Answers will vary. 3. change, alter; 4. Provide information about hair.

Page 50

1. right, critical, crucial, pivotal; 2. A, C; 3. Answers will vary. 4. Answers will vary.

Page 51

Day 1: The brainstorming activity should contain various ideas or words related to the topic while trying to persuade. **Day 2:** The first draft should contain ideas taken from the brainstorming activity. **Day 3:** The next draft should show improvements in organization and detail. **Day 4:** The final draft should show proofreading marks where needed.

Page 52

The content of writing samples will vary. Check to be sure that students have correctly completed all of the earlier steps in the writing process and have followed instructions for publishing their work.

Page 53

Day 1: 1. Clara Brown; 2. nonfiction; 3. sh; 4. Answers will vary. **Day 2:** 1. free African Americans; 2. census; 3. Answers will vary. 4. Answers will vary. **Day 3:** 1. free; 2. to prove they were not runaway slaves; 3. to earn money because she could not pay for the trip; 4. to find her daughter; **Day 4:** 1. Yes. She made money with her laundry business. 2. She helped ex-slaves move to Colorado. 3. come together again; 4. Answers will vary.

Page 54

1. half; 2. oxen; 3. B; 4. Answers will vary. 5. Answers will vary.

Page 55

Day 1: The brainstorming activity should contain various ideas or words related to writing a biography. **Day 2:** The first draft should contain ideas taken from the brainstorming activity. **Day 3:** The next draft should show improvements in organization and detail. **Day 4:** The final draft should show proofreading marks where needed.

Page 56

The content of writing samples will vary. Check to be sure that students have correctly completed all of the earlier steps in the writing process and have followed instructions for publishing their work.

Page 57

Day 1: 1. James Beckwourth and fur trading; 2. fur trading; 3. yes; 4. People of different races worked together. **Day 2:** 1. 15; 2. ride horses, work the land, cook, fish, and track game; 3. Answers will vary. 4. East, Midwest, West; **Day 3:** 1. B; 2. He learned to trap beaver and otter.; 3. no; 4. go ahead of the group to see if the trail is safe and worthwhile; **Day 4:** 1. Sierra Nevadas; 2. blacksmith, trapper, scout, mountain man; 3. Answers will vary. 4. Answers will vary.

Page 58

1. Answers will vary. 2. because they were free and they could go to Texas and work for pay; 3. Yes. He won every event at the rodeo. 4. He was interested in archeology and loved to hunt for fossils. 5. Caucasian, Spanish, African American

Page 59

Day 1: 1. C; 2. (circled) He, our; 3. (inserted) period; 4. (circled) lies; **Day 2:** 1. C; 2. (circled) Effects, except; 3. (inserted) question mark; 4. (circled) lain; **Day 3:** 1. B; 2. (circled) us, his; 3. (inserted) exclamation points; 4. (circled) laid; **Day 4:** 1. A; 2. (circled) I, her; 3. (inserted) period; 4. (circled) Lie

Page 60

1. B; 2. C; 3. C; 4. (circled) she; except; 5. (circled) us, our; 6. (inserted) period; 7. (inserted) period; 8. (inserted) question mark; 9. (circled) lies; 10. (circled) lay

Page 61

Day 1: 1. It is a legend about the Cherokee rose. 2. Yes. It tells that the Cherokee were Native Americans who were forced to move from Georgia to the Indian Territory. 3. no; 4. Answers will vary. **Day 2:** 1. They had to walk. 2. no; 3. the Cherokee mothers; 4. There was not enough food and water, and many of the Cherokee died. **Day 3:** 1. the chiefs; 2. They asked the Great One for a way to make the mothers feel better. 3. Answers will vary. 4. Answers will vary. **Day 4:** 1. a white rose; 2. It grows where a mother's tear falls; 3. White petals stand for the mothers' tears, gold center for the gold that was taken from the tribes, and seven leaves for the seven groups that walked along the Trail of Tears. 4. Answers will vary.

Page 62

1. The settlers wanted the gold found on the land. 2. no; 3. The trail on which the Native Americans traveled to the Indian Territory; 4. Answers will vary.

Page 63

Day 1: The brainstorming activity should contain various ideas or words related to the topic. **Day 2:** The first draft should contain ideas taken from the brainstorming activity. **Day 3:** The next draft should show improvements in organization and detail including using proper letter writing format. **Day 4:** The final draft should show proofreading marks where needed.

Page 64

The content of writing samples will vary. Check to be sure that students have correctly completed all of the earlier steps in the writing process and have followed instructions for publishing their work.

Page 65

Day 1: 1. It will be about George Washington Carver. 2. Incredible; 3. no; 4. President George Washington; **Day 2:** 1. He spent time collecting flowers and plants. 2. He taught himself to read.; 3. He was 10 years old when he left the plantation to live on his own. 4. Answers will vary. **Day 3:** 1. no; 2. He refused to give up; 3. science; 4. He was an excellent student. **Day 4:** 1. He discovered more than 300 uses for the peanut plant. 2. Answers will vary. 3. Answers will vary. 4. Answers will vary.

Page 66
1. A machine was invented to make de-seeding cotton easier. 2. The cotton growers brought in more slaves. 3. Eli Whitney was brilliant. 4. The invention of the cotton gin made slavery grow in the South.

Page 67
Day 1: 1. (underlined with three short lines) did, *around, world, days,* academy, award; 2. (underlined) cheered for our favorite team, (circled) cheered; 3. "The Olympic Games were held in Stockholm, Sweden," replied Valerie. 4. due, week; **Day 2:** 1. (underlined with three short lines) robert burns, auld, lang, syne; 2. (underlined) dropped one more quarter into the machine, (circled) dropped; 3. Monica yelled, "Wow, did you see that car"? 4. eight, flowers; **Day 3:** 1. (underlined with three short lines) does, grandpa, *chicago, sun, times, chicago, tribune;* 2. (underlined) examined the jacket carefully, (circled) examined; 3. "Look out!" screamed Andrew. 4. sent, aunt; **Day 4:** 1. (underlined with three short lines) we're, Italian, Friday, *strega, nona;* 2. (underlined) is a frisky animal, (circled) is; 3. Bobbi, our class president, took charge of today's meeting. 4. Two, fair

Page 68
1. (underlined with three short lines) i, *the, life, cycle, book, cats;* period at end of sentence; 2. (underlined with three short lines) will, judge, j.t., ormand; question mark at end of sentence; 3. (underlined with three short lines) dad, *los, angeles, times,* dave; quotation marks, comma after morning, period at end of sentence; 4. (underlined with three short lines) dions, deli, turkish, penny; quotation marks, apostrophe in Dion's, comma after candy, period at end of sentence; 5. (underlined) asked for volunteers, (circled) asked; 6. (underlined) ate all of the seeds; (circled) ate; 7. (underlined) are in the same race, (circled) are; 8. (circled) sent, flowers; 9. (circled) two, weeks, due; 10. (circled) eight, aunts

Page 69
Day 1: 1. the Underground Railroad; 2. support; 3. the Underground Railroad; 4. conductors (people who helped slaves escape) and passengers (slaves); **Day 2:** 1. compares the Underground Railroad to a train; 2. both move people; 3. the Underground Railroad does not move on tracks; 4. Answers will vary. **Day 3:** 1. conductors; 2. Harriet Tubman and Levi Coffin; 3. to guide slaves and provide supplies; 4. Harriet Tubman was an escaped slave. **Day 4:** 1. getting freedom for slaves; 2. Answers will vary. 3. 35 years; 4. Answers will vary.

Page 70
1. They sold for a higher price. 2. She earned money to buy her freedom. 3. a quilt that told a family's story; 4. because it told their story

Page 71
Day 1: The brainstorming activity should contain various ideas or words related to the topic completing the graphic organizer. **Day 2:** The first draft should contain ideas taken from the graphic organizer. **Day 3:** The next draft should show improvements in organization and detail. **Day 4:** The final draft should show proofreading marks where needed.

Page 72
The content of writing samples will vary. Check to be sure that students have correctly completed all of the earlier steps in the writing process and have followed instructions for publishing their work.

Page 73
Day 1: 1. It is about Aboriginal art; 2. Australia; 3. They were hunters and gatherers and skilled artists. 4. Native Americans; **Day 2:** 1. from the earth, tree bark, and plants; 2. black; 3. no; 4. Gypsum is a mineral used in both. **Day 3:** 1. rocks and didgeridoos; 2. Large. It is made from a hollowed-out log. 3. yes; 4. They were made from logs. **Day 4:** 1. rocks, didgeridoos, and themselves; 2. It links them to the land and nature. 3. dance, sing, and tell stories; 4. They paint themselves.

Page 74

1. The time that the world was created; 2. Yes. It has been passed down by the elders. 3. They are symmetrical and include arcs, circles, ovals, and lines. 4. Answers will vary.

Page 75

Day 1: The brainstorming activity should contain various ideas or words related to the topic. **Day 2:** The first draft should contain ideas taken from the brainstorming activity. **Day 3:** The next draft should show improvements in organization and detail. **Day 4:** The final draft should show proofreading marks where needed.

Page 76

The content of writing samples will vary. Check to be sure that students have correctly completed all of the earlier steps in the writing process and have followed instructions for publishing their work.

Page 77

Day 1: 1. gh; 2. observed; 3. Each year, the citizens of the United States celebrate two holidays to remember men and women who fought in wars to preserve their freedom. 4. Memorial Day; **Day 2:** 1. birthplace; 2. a place where a body is buried; 3. May 5, 1866; 4. Answers will vary. **Day 3:** 1. Decoration Day; 2. slavery; 3. Answers will vary. 4. Answers will vary. **Day 4:** 1. sh; 2. C; 3. first, now; 4. United States, France, Great Britain, Russia, and Italy

Page 78

1. prefix – en; root – light; suffixes – en, ing; 2. A; 3. the symbolism of the Statue of Liberty; 4. the seven rays on the crown; 5. Answers will vary.

Page 79

Day 1: The brainstorming activity should contain various ideas or words related to the topic to be researched. **Day 2:** The first draft should contain ideas taken from the brainstorming activity. **Day 3:** The next draft should show improvements in organization and detail. **Day 4:** The final draft should show proofreading marks where needed.

Page 80

The content of writing samples will vary. Check to be sure that students have correctly completed all of the earlier steps in the writing process and have followed instructions for publishing their work.

Page 81

Day 1: 1. tarantula; 2. Answers will vary but may include small, little, bald, and smooth. 3. C; 4. Answers will vary. **Day 2:** 1. (circled) catch; 2. A; 3. Its poison cannot kill a human. 4. its poison; **Day 3:** 1. no; 2. timid, afraid; 3. They might feel a sting. 4. B; **Day 4:** 1. (circled) itself, its, which, its, stiff, skin; 2. injury; 3. stiff, tiny; 4. The tiny hairs could hurt your eyes.

Page 82

1. It eats flies. 2. meat-eater; 3. To get information about the Venus flytrap; 4. Answers will vary.

Page 83

Day 1: The brainstorming activity should contain various ideas or words related to the topic being researched. **Day 2:** The first draft should contain ideas taken from the brainstorming activity. **Day 3:** The next draft should show improvements in organization and detail. **Day 4:** The final draft should show proofreading marks where needed.

Page 84

The content of writing samples will vary. Check to be sure that students have correctly completed all of the earlier steps in the writing process and have followed instructions for publishing their work.

Page 85

Day 1: 1. broth; 2. add; 3. the sloth's; 4. poem; **Day 2:** 1. keep living; 2. They live in tropical rain forests. 3. the sloth; rain forests; 4. No. They need to live in a rain forest; **Day 3:** 1. downright; 2. They are slow. They have a brownish-green furry coat. 3. a furry animal living in a tree; 4. Answers will vary. **Day 4:** 1. herbivore; 2. They sleep through the day and eat plants. 3. eat; 4. A

Page 86

1. a squirrel; 2. a rabbit; 3. C; 4. Answers will vary.

Page 87
Day 1: The brainstorming activity should contain various ideas or words related to the topic being researched. **Day 2:** The first draft should contain ideas taken from the brainstorming activity.
Day 3: The next draft should show improvements in organization and detail. **Day 4:** The final draft should show proofreading marks where needed.

Page 88
The content of writing samples will vary. Check to be sure that students have correctly completed all of the earlier steps in the writing process and have followed instructions for publishing their work.